PICTORIAL HISTORY
of
PAISLEY

David Rowand F.S.A. (Scot).

COVER:
"Gauze Street 1888" by Patrick Downie
David Rowand Collection.

First Published in 1993
by Alloway Publishing Ltd.,
Darvel Ayrshire.

Second Edition printed 1997

Printed in Scotland
by Walker & Connell Ltd.,
Hastings Square,
Darvel, Ayrshire.

ISBN No. 0-907526-55-1

PICTORIAL HISTORY
of
PAISLEY

David Rowand F.S.A. (Scot).

Alloway Publishing

INTRODUCTION

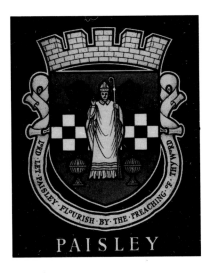

It could be said that Paisley gave the cold, shivering world, the Paisley Shawl to wrap itself up and keep warm. Paisley's own colourful tapestry has been woven by countless 'Buddies' over the centuries. The heritage they left were the buildings and streets of the town, the traditions and customs, the written histories, drawings and photographs, all made depicting the Paisley of their time. In this book, is a selection of material, much of it new and previously unpublished, drawn from a wide area, as can be seen from the select bibliography. For their help in the preparation of this book I thank, in particular; Jan A Brown, who assiduously typed the manuscripts and gave sound advice; the staff of Paisley Museum for their help and the use of the museum's collection without which this book would have been far less colourful; Paul Weatherall, V Reilly, David Roberts and A Gildea of Paisley Museum; K Hinshalwood and A Scott of Paisley Library. In addition, I thank the following for their help, present and past: B Aiken; the Barrett Family; M Baxter; S Baxter; the Bohemian Club; J Borthwick; B Brennan; J A Brown; J Chapman; J Craig; A Deayton; B Duncan; Mrs R Fairbrother; M Ferguson; A Gardner Ltd; Glasgow District Museums; Glasgow Transport Museum; Mr & Mrs J McGoogan; Mrs Margt. Gregg; F Hardy Studios; Jim Hyslop, Alloway Publishing; Barclay Lennie Fine Art; the Connell Family; E McCracken; Mr & Mrs McKay; Ken Mackay; A Mackenzie of McDougal Bros; J McLachlan; D Malcolm; P Marshall; Dr H Munro; the Old Paisley Society; Outram Archives; C Payne; The Postmaster General, Canada; Mr & Mrs R Reid; K Robertson; Miss J C Rodger; Mrs N Rowand; the Scottish Film Archive; the Scottish National Portrait Gallery, Edinburgh; W Shanks; C Souter; E Speirs; Bob Walker; Fulton Walker; Prof. F Walker; Mr & Mrs I Winning. This book is in memory of Norman M Rowand, my father, and dedicated to Mum, Mary my wife, Alison and Christopher our children and to the sons and daughters of Paisley at home and abroad.

Paisley
Scotland

David Rowand
1993

HISTORICAL SKETCH

EARLY BEGINNINGS

Strong local traditions exist that the two hills of Castlehead and Oakshaw had early forms of fortification. At Castlehead, early, if scant, remains of a medieval hill-ring fort have been found. In the 17th century, at Oakshaw, there were large remains still visible. These were described as 'three fosses and dykes of earth so great that men on horseback could not see over them'. That these two sites contained Roman remains is unlikely, since no such finds have been unearthed there. Although it is an attractive idea there is no evidence to support the belief, so beloved by Victorian historians, that Paisley was the Vindogara of Ptolemy's ancient map.

Paisley's real birthplace was at Seedhill, the land adjoining the Hammills waterfall. There the River Cart could be easily forded and Seedhill, as its later name implied, had good fertile soil. This is where Paisley's earliest cleared settlement would have been.

According to legend, in about 560 AD, an Irish monk came to this settlement and founded a Celtic church. His name was Mirin. This holy man, after completing his mission, in what is now Strathclyde, 'fell asleep in the Lord at Paisley' and a church was built dedicated to his memory. Until the Reformation, a small building called St Mirin's Chapel stood in Seedhill. Connected to it was a graveyard and a priest's house. This may or may not have been connected with St Mirin's original church.

THE MONASTERY

In 1163, Walter Fitzalan, High Steward of Scotland, great-grandson of Alan, Steward of Dol in Britanny, drew up the charter of foundation to build a church in Paisley.

He had been gifted large tracts of land in Renfrewshire, by King David I. In Renfrew, he built his castle and at Paisley he built a house of devotion. Cluniac monks from the Priory of Wenlock, Shropshire, took up residence in the new church in about 1172. The workings of this Cluniac order would have been familiar to Walter, through his family ties with Shropshire. After all, his brother was Sheriff of that County and Lord of Oswestrie and had himself been a pious benefactor of religious houses.

The site chosen for the new priory was ideal. The Seedhill area had previously been cultivated and already supported a corn mill which was to be among the first gifts to the new church. Good building material was near at hand; white sandstone abounded at Ladykirk nearby; lime from Blackhall, together with oak and beech from the forests of Hunterhill and Fereneze were within easy reach. However, the most impor-

tant factor in choosing this site, at least to the pious mind of the 12th century, was that a shrine dedicated to St Mirin already existed at Seedhill. This would give the new church a religious provenance and ensure that it became a place of pilgrimage in medieval Scotland.

In 1245, through further gifts and patronage under the High Stewards, the Priory of Paisley was raised to the rank of an Abbey. This was distinction indeed, as only the mother house at Cluny had previously claimed this honour! From the transumpt of Pope Clement IV in 1265, we learn that Paisley Abbey owned twenty-eight churches. That, together with benefactions and revenues, made it one of the wealthiest in the kingdom. In 1307, the English burned the Abbey. The 'Black Book of Paisley' records that the 'Monastery was left with nothing but blackened walls'. This was retribution for the part the Abbey played during the Wars of Independence, particularly as 'The Wallace' and 'The Bruce' had close family connections with the Stewards and their Abbey. Indeed in 1308 Bruce was absolved of the murder of Red Comyn by the Abbot of Paisley.

After Bannockburn, around 1317, sporadic repairs to the Church began. In 1334, Pope Benedict XII gave the Abbot of Paisley, the insignia of mitre and ring. This gave the Church episcopal jurisdiction over the large, widespread numbers of churches in its possession.

THE GREAT ABBOTS

Abbot Lithgow (1384-1433) continued the work of rebuilding the Church. Purchases of glass for the choir windows

Black Book of Paisley records fire of 1307.

6

are recorded between 1389-90. During this time King Robert III made the Abbey lands into a Regality, giving the Abbot kingly right over his vassals. Lithgow, an able administrator, successfully fought off claims of jurisdiction over him, made by the Bishop of Glasgow.

Abbot Thomas Morow (1433-1444) is recorded as being more interested in spiritual matters than temporal.

Great Seal of Abbey

Abbot Tervas (1445-1459) proved to be a splendid Abbot, despite buying his appointment. Widely travelled abroad, he duly returned to his monastery with rich jewels, plate, ornate church vestments and the 'stateliest tabernacle in all Scotland and the most costly.' He also obtained a charter from King James II, which allowed wine to be sold in the Abbey premises. The revenues from this may have helped the building fund, as well as catering for pilgrims. Incidentally, from his foreign visit, he also brought back retainers called Algeo, which introduced the later name Algie into Renfrewshire.

Abbot Crichton (1459-1472) began the rental book of the Abbey, which today is a valuable source of mediaeval methods of land tenure. For example, in 1460, an entry reads - 'the place which is called Nether Crossflat is let to Thomas Hector, sculptor ..... the said Thomas will hold himself ready and prepared to the said Abbot and convent in all that concerns his art as a sculptor.'

Seal of Abbot Schaw

Abbot George Schaw (1473-1498) was the most remarkable of all. He was both a builder and an administrator. The larger part of the conventual buildings, now known as the Place of Paisley, though much altered, we owe to him. During his time of office, in 1485, he erected the most handsome wall in Scotland around the Abbey grounds. It was a mile long, adorned at intervals with beautiful statues and carved inscriptions. The great gatehouse, built by Abbot Tervas, was surmounted by Abbot Schaw's tower. The name of Wallneuk reminds us today that one corner of the wall was situated near the junction of Lawn Street and Incle Street.

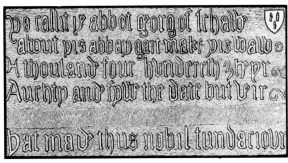

Inscription from Abbot Schaw's Abbey Wall, 1485

PAISLEY BURGH

In 1488, young King James IV granted Abbot Schaw, his friend at Court, a charter to form the village into a Burgh. This charter was confirmed by the Abbot to Paisley in 1490. The following year, under direction from the Pope, Schaw absolved this young, remorseful King for any part he may have had in the murder of his father, King James III, at Sauchieburn. The solemn ceremony took place in Paisley Abbey in 1491.

Abbot Schaw lost no time in giving his new Burgh its symbols of office. He appointed the first town council and presented the town with its first tolbooth, which contained a courtroom and jail. It was built on the High Street/Moss Street corner. Nearby, the proud citizens of Paisley erected their market cross, no doubt encouraged by Abbot Schaw. Soon afterwards, the men of the Royal Burgh of Renfrew arrived and, eager to destroy this new rival in trade, threw down Paisley's market cross. They also carried off quantities of beef and white cloth in lieu of customs due. Up to that time, Renfrew had claimed duties on all goods sold in Paisley and had done so illegally since 1451, the year that Paisley, by virtue of its Charter of Regality, was no longer subject to Renfrew. Not to be outdone, the Paisley men raided Renfrew to destroy its market cross. Renfrew took legal action against Paisley. Abbot Schaw, always protective of his Burgh of Paisley, threatened to sue Renfrew for reparation of back-dated dues, claimed since 1451. Renfrew backed down.

MEDIEVAL VILLAGE

Paisley, as a village, had evolved over the centuries, in tandem with the monastery, but it was confined, with the exception of Seedhill, to the west bank of the River Cart. Its early function, besides providing land revenues to the Abbey, was to provide men, labour and materials.

Paisley's early appearance consisted of a High Street whose sporadic little buildings ended at Townhead. Beyond this were the Lands of Priorscroft, Wellmeadow and Broomlands. The High Street was built on a developable mid-point contour, between the Oakshaw Ridge to the north, and on the slope terminated by the St Mirin Burn to the south.

Moss Street, skirting around the Oakshaw Ridge, led to the Barnyard on the west (Oakshaw) and to the pasture land at Nethercommon on the north. St Mirin's Wynd, then a narrow little vennel led diagonally from the Cross, over what is now Dunn Square, towards the River Cart. From the bottom of this Wynd, Causeyside, with its cluster of little houses, continued southwards as a 'causied' or paved road, as far as the Longait (Canal Street).

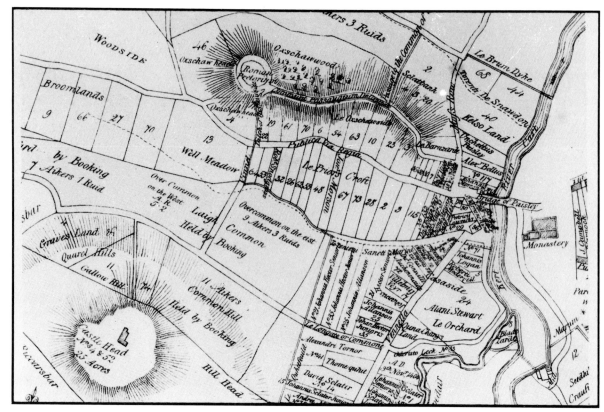

Map of Paisley 1490-1545

Just as there had been three classes of individuals in the medieval village — tenants, bondsmen, and natives (the latter two were virtual slaves), so there were three classes of land use.

First was the burghal land, where tenants or burgesses built their houses. This land, held by tenure of booking and not by infeftment, was unique to Paisley and was to remain in use until 1927! Secondly, outfield land at Seedhill, Oakshaw, Wellmeadow, Broomlands, Castlehead and Sneddon was used for cultivation. Thirdly, Common Land, at the Moss, Underwood, and the Laigh Common (North of Canal Street) was shared by the Abbey and the villagers as pasture land.

Abbot Schaw died in 1498 and was succeeded by his nephew, Abbot Robert Schaw (1498-1525). He set about a further rebuilding of the Abbey, as it had suffered serious damage in a pre-1498 fire. This same fire probably allowed the independent building, in 1499, of the St Mirin Chapel, using part of the old south transept of the Abbey. Its erection also indicated the rise of wealthy town burgesses, for it was to this class that James Crawford, its founder and benefactor, belonged.

Abbot Hamilton (1525-1553) built a central tower in the Abbey, but, towards the end of his abbacy, it collapsed and destroyed the choir. In 1547, while retaining his abbacy at Paisley, Hamilton was appointed to the highest rank of the Church — Archbishop of St Andrews, Primate of Scotland. He was a noted opponent of the reformer John Knox and a close advisor and adherent of Mary, Queen of Scots. For opposing the Reformation and refusing to accept the new order, Archbishop Hamilton was executed in Stirling in 1571,

He is buried in Paisley Abbey, where there is a tablet to his memory.

In 1553, Abbot Hamilton had resigned the abbacy, His nephew, Claud Hamilton, a child of ten, inherited the Abbey and its lands as a Protestant baron. In 1587, when the town became a secular Burgh of Barony, Claud became Lord Paisley. Claud's son became Earl of Abercorn in 1603.

REFORMATION

Knox, the reformer, described Paisley as 'a nest of papistrie' as it was one of the last places in Scotland to turn to the new religion. When Glencairn swept into the town with his rabble of reformers, they burnt what was left of the Abbey and looted and destroyed its medieval splendours. This was Paisley's first taste of Protestantism. No wonder, that the first Protestant minister to arrive in the town was 'locked out' of the Abbey! Succeeding ministers could not find accommodation in the town. One even accused its citizens of having 'manifest vices' accompanied by 'menacing and boasting' and suffering from 'a contempt of discipline'!

It was to the new religion, however, that the Grammar School owed its foundation in 1576.

By 1596, the town council, now advocates of Protestantism, decree that people found playing, selling meat or drink on the Sabbath, or abstaining from Sabbath church services should be fined. Failing this they should be held in the stocks for twenty hours!

The most organised, yet troublesome, trades people in the town were the fleshers. They formed themselves into a trade syndicate in 1596, which enabled them to control meat prices.

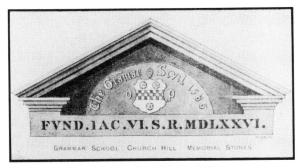

Grammar School Stone, 1586

Silver Bells, Paisley Races, 1620

The Council did not like this, but only succeeded in breaking the monopoly in 1666!

A ROYAL VISIT

In 1617, the town bailies on hearing of a proposed Royal visit from King James VI, pleaded poverty and claimed that they could not entertain him in the sumptuous manner befitting a king. When the King arrived he did not enter the Burgh, but instead was entertained in the great hall of 'Nobill Abercorn', the Place of Paisley. The Queen's previous visit in 1597, had caused the town great expense! The bailies had to pay a Glasgow painter to draw 'designs' (possibly heraldic) in the Abbey Kirk and employ a wright to repair the town's port.

DISEASE

Leprosy is first mentioned in the town records in 1601. Plague, first recorded in 1456, was a frequent visitor, with further outbreaks taking place in 1588, 1600, 1602, 1604 and 1645. During the later epidemics, the Council sensibly ordered the town's ports to be closed and strangers turned away. In 1647, Glasgow University lodged for two months in Paisley, to avoid the plague then ravaging Glasgow.

17th CENTURY PAISLEY

The town at this time had a few important buildings. The tollbooth at the Cross had been rebuilt in 1610 and a new clock added in 1647. The High Street had an almshouse or hospital founded in 1618, and contained some important town houses. These were the 'tenements' built by Lord Sempill (1580), Cochran of Craigmuir (1608), the Family of Ferguslie (1594) and the 'House of All Saints' which had belonged to the monastery.

At School Wynd, stood the Grammar School. At the top of St Mirin's Wynd, tenements called the 'Paisley Tak', 'St Catherine's tile tenement', and 'The Chamberlain's House' were located. The 'Paisley Tak' had belonged to Richard Brigton in 1500. He had served as a buckler to the monastery.

The Chamberlain's House was built in 1471, by Sir John Mouss, chamberlain to the monastery. This house later became the property of John Sempill of Beltrees, "vulgarly known at the royal court as 'The Danser'." His wife, Mary Livingstone, was one of the 'Four Maries' of Mary, Queen of Scots.

In 1658, the magistrates of Paisley bought the superiority of the Burgh from the Earl of Dundonald. This step alone ensured unhindered future physical development of the Burgh by the Burgh authorities and no-one else. In 1666, a charter of confirmation and resignation by King Charles II in favour of the Burgh, became the 'Magna Carta' of the town. It made the bailies, town council, and community their own masters. Paisley, in 1695, had 460 houses and a population of just over 1000 people over the age of sixteen. Of these, 66 were weavers, with a further 33 weavers in the landward area. The number employed in this trade would suggest, that the cloth produced, was for a market wider than Paisley. In addition to weavers, there were 41 merchants, 33 shoemakers, and 21 maltsters. Beside the usual professions, such as doctors, writers, and apothecaries, the town boasted of having two wigmakers.

Paisley showed typical caution, by investing only £100 in the doomed Darien Scheme of 1698.

18th CENTURY PAISLEY

Lord Sempill's House, Paisley High Street

The town, described, in 1705, as a 'better town and more central than Renfrew' gained the County Sheriff Court. This act alone heralded Paisley's growing importance, for it was to become Renfrewshire's leading town.

Just prior to the Act of Union in 1707, Paisley sent a written protest to the Scots Parliament in Edinburgh. However, when the Act was passed, the town accepted it calmly.

Paisley, in 1710, was 'a very pleasant and well-built little town; plentifully provided with all sorts of grain, fruits, coals, peats, fishes, and what else is proper for the comfortable use of man or can be expected in any other place of the Kingdom'.

It is no wonder, when trade and prosperity was threatened by the 1715 Rebellion, Paisley supported the Hanoverian Government. Apart from forming a town guard, young

Blackston House

volunteers, enticed by the offer of free burgess-ship, were enrolled, mustered and trained as soldiers. Of the 140 volunteers so raised, some fought bravely at Sheriffmuir, while others succeeded in quelling the troublesome Rob Roy MacGregor and his marauding clansmen. At Loch Lomond, the Paisley Volunteers, by the simple expedient of stealing the Clan's boats, removed the threat of Highland invasion to the town and its neighbourhood.

Equally spirited was Paisley's loyalty in the 1745 Rebellion. In 1746, the town woke up to find that two of its senior bailies had been taken hostage in Glasgow, by the Jacobite forces stationed there. A sum of £1000 had been levied on Paisley. If not paid, the town was to be pillaged and looted, as had the nearby mansion of Blackston, the house of a distinguished Hanoverian soldier, Alexander Napier. With Highlanders on the town's doorstep, the town panicked. Some wealthier citizens made out their last wills and testaments. Local farmers hid their cattle in the Lochwinnoch hills. After negotiations with the Jacobites, Paisley beat the demand down

to £500, and even that money was borrowed! The town was saved. The Paisley Volunteers, led by their ensign John Renfrew fought successfully for King and Country at the Battle of Falkirk in 1746.

TEXTILE PAISLEY

At the time of the Act of Union, the town had about 100 looms specialising in the production of 'Bengals' — imitation striped muslins — and making coarse linen checks.

With free trade opened up to England, and encouraged by Paisley packmen taking the town's products there, the weaving trade expanded. Production moved to checked and spotted handkerchiefs, and plain, striped, spotted and figured lawns, that together with linen and gauze, proved a commercial success.

Silk gauze manufacture was introduced to the town in 1759, by Humphrey Fulton. He established around 600 looms at Maxwellton where, 'by inventive spirit, patient application of the workmen, and the skill and taste of the masters', silk gauze was produced. These soon excelled the products of London's Spitalfield weavers, then considered 'Kings of silk weaving'. A number of firms came to Paisley, so that, by 1773, there were 876 looms producing silk and 557 producing linen.

The growth in industry was matched by the expansion of the town. In 1779, a new town was built on the East bank of the River Cart. The new streets were given names to reflect the town's industry, for example Cotton Street, Silk Street, Gauze Street and Lawn Street. This new town was described thus, 'the elegant appearances of the grand houses on both sides of Gauze Street, strikes the attention of the travelling stranger. Most of these houses are three storeys high, of good ashlar work, with doors and cornices ornamented with different orders'.

The town's population inclusive of the Newtown had reached 24,000. In 1821, Paisley ranked third in size in Scotland after Edinburgh and Glasgow.

In the town's booming weaving industry, linen had evolved into lawn, cotton into muslin and silk into gauze. A Paisley weaver could tackle anything. 'Nothing in their own branch of weaving was too hard for them'. He was also his own master, taking his leisure as pleased him. Owning his own loom, he could work his own hours. It was to be noted that, while a weaver's web was for sale, his time was not! Soon all this was to change.

In 1805, James Paterson, an Edinburgh manufacturer, employed Paisley weavers to produce the newly-fashionable, Kashmir-type shawls. He knew full well that some of the highly-skilled weavers of Paisley, out of work because of trade recession, were capable of handling this delicate work. Soon the Paisley textile trade took up this lucrative shawl manufacture and applied themselves to it with vigour and inventiveness.

Initially, drawlooms were used, so to some degree designs woven were limited and did-not always display the pine patterns. Angola shawls and cotton 'fur' shawls featured in the town's weavers' early repertoire.

Alexander Buchanan, a Paisley manufacturer, is credited with producing the first 'Cheneille' shawls, sold in the shops as 'velvet on silk' — beautiful specimens of the weavers' art. Being unwashable, they fell out of fashion. Robert Kerr, in the

A Paisley Weaver & draw boy

1820s, was producing all-wool shawls, known locally as 'thibet shawls'.

Shawl production valued at £1,000.000 had been achieved in 1834. Trade was prosperous. Even Queen Adelaide wore a 'cabille' shawl woven on the town's harness looms, by John Roxburgh & Son. It was the first successful application in the country of a harness loom to an entirely all-wool fabric.

Two Paisley dyers, Scroggie and Gilchrist, put paid to London and Edinburgh dyers by producing locally made dyed silks and all sorts of other cloth.

The Jacquard loom appeared in Paisley as early as the 1820s. By the 1830s, shawl production on a grand scale took off. Design became more complex. Specialists, such as beamers and warpers, who were needed to set-up the complex looms, began to erode the individual weaver's independence.

Lady with Paisley shawl

Besides, many 'gentlemen weavers' could not afford the capital outlay required for a Jacquard loom, let alone house it in their low-roofed cottages. The unmitigated success of the Jacquard led to a system of factory production in the town.

Parallel to woven shawls, Paisley also produced printed varieties. This method of production came to Paisley later than to other competitors, allowing its operatives to build and profit from the experience of others. Contrary to popular belief, these printed shawls were initially expensive items and required printers, block cutters and a design team, just as highly skilled as the weavers. Paisley had, therefore, two strings to her shawl-making bow.

TRADE DEPRESSION

The shawl trade, however, had its periods of depression and slump, due mainly to the vagaries of fashion. Over-production of similar designs made the shawl less exclusive as a fashion article and therefore unpopular in fashionable circles, who regarded the designs as 'common'.

Between 1841 and 1843, the town suffered her worst ever trade depression, when half of the town's textile firms failed. In 1842, some 15,000 weavers and their families were receiving relief from public subscription and from under-cover, Government sources. The Government had not forgotten the awesome reputation that Paisley held during the Radical Riots in 1819 and 1820. These might well repeat themselves in a depressed, out-of-work town. Paisley did not riot, but became bankrupt in 1842 despite the sympathy and support of Queen Victoria who purchased a number of Paisley shawls that year, which led to a brief trade revival. Only in 1872, would Paisley become solvent again.

In the 1850s, Paisley Shawls reigned supreme. Mass production, price undercutting, pirating of designs, organisation of labour and marketing ousted other centres of shawl manufacture, such as Edinburgh. At this period, 'Paisley Shawls' and 'Paisley Pattern' became synonymous, though only the latter survives today.

In the 1870s, ladies' fashions changed. The style of dress was for a tight-fitting bodice and a bustled skirt. The flowing lines of the shawl looked incongruous with the bustle and it quickly fell out of fashion. To try and save the day, the remaining Paisley looms produced tartan shawls and stoles and even made ponchos for South America; but the trade was doomed. The shawl trade could not last forever.

Brown & Polson Paisley flour

OTHER INDUSTRIES

It was not weaving that was to sustain local industries during the later part of the 19th century, but industries which had been ancillary to that trade.

Starch paste had been used to stiffen warp threads on the town's looms. From the supply of this commodity a whole industry grew up. Brown & Polson, established in 1842, first at Thrushcraigs and later at the Royal Starch Works, Falside Road, became a household name in 'Patent Corn Flour' introduced in 1856. By the 1920s, it was the world's largest producer of cornflour.

Built on the success of his 'shawl cropping machines', introduced in 1868, A F Craig founded a large industry, which produced such items as carpet-weaving looms, oil distillation plant and sugar-cane crushing plant. Its Caledonia Foundry, in its day, could handle the largest castings in Scotland.

Templeton, a Paisley weaver, founded a huge carpet manufacturing business in Glasgow.

Dyeing, cloth finishing, and other off-shoot industries produced a plethora of large factories throughout the town - for example, William Fulton & Sons, Glenfield; Pollock & Cochrane, Thrushcraigs; and J J McCallum, Laighpark.

The most important industry to sustain the town after the demise of the shawl trade was threadmaking. This occupation in Paisley was as old as weaving, the two being irretrievably linked. Making thread in Paisley, at least on a commercial basis, had a curious beginning.

Bargarran Thread

About 1725, the making of white stitching thread was introduced to Johnstone by a Mrs Millar of Bargarran (nee Christian Shaw). Through a Glasgow merchant, who sometimes visited the Dutch port of Campvere, she obtained a smuggled thread twisting mill, a small machine which ran twelve bobbins at a time. Soon she was a commercial success. Her thread marketed as 'Bargarran' was as good as, if not better than any that was imported from Holland, then the major supplier of thread to this country. In time, her assistants 'leaked out' her production methods. Linen thread manufacture was soon set up at nearby Paisley.

Mrs Millar of Bargarran, nee Christian Shaw, is best remembered as the infamous daughter of a Lowland laird, who claimed she had been afflicted by the Devil. She convinced the Paisley Presbytery through her machinations that it was so and thereby, in 1697, caused the cruel death of two men and four women accused of witchcraft. One of the accused managed to kill himself in Paisley Tollbooth Jail. The other five were strangled and burnt on the Gallow Green and buried at the cross-roads of Maxwellton Street and what is now George Street. A horse shoe, until recently, marked the spot of the burials.

After pirating Mrs Millar's thread-making process, linen thread production in the town mushroomed. In 1774, Paisley had 93 mills (ie machines) in operation. A fifth of Scotland's thread output was based in Paisley in 1784. With the invention of Crompton's 'Mule' in 1779, Paisley manufacturers gained access to fine, clean, smooth cotton yarn, which they easily converted into three or six cord cable thread almost as strong as linen. 'King Cotton' had arrived.

THE CLARK FAMILY

The history of the cotton spool trade is synonomous with the Clark family. In 1753, William Clark, a farmer at Dykebar, died, leaving a large family. Too young to work the farm, they took employment in nearby Paisley. One son, James Clark, set up business in Cotton Street as a weaver's furnisher and heddle twine maker. The heddles were made of fine silk, as that part had to be very smooth. The supply of silk from Europe dried up, due, in the main, to Napoleon's famous Berlin Decree in 1806. This predicament caused James Clark's brother, Patrick, to turn his attention to perfecting a smooth, fine, cotton thread to supersede silk.

The new product was first marketed in 1812. Operating as J & J Clark, the brothers erected a factory at Seedhill. James Clark is credited with the invention of the wooden spool or bobbin. His customers were charged a half-penny for the spool. This was refundable when the empty spool was returned to him. Up to that time, thread was sold in hanks or skeins.

Robert Paul, his wood turner, set up his shop where the Town Hall now stands. The Seedhill Mills continued to prosper under the Clark family. Most of the factory output was for the home market, although they later erected a large mill at Newark, New Jersey. The company adopted the anchor trademark to thwart their many imitators. They formed a limited liability company in 1896 and amalgamated with their arch rivals J & P Coats, that same year.

COATS FAMILY

James Coats (1774-1857), originally a 'cork' or manufacturer in the tambouring trade, formed a partnership with James Whyte to produce 'Canton Crepe'. For several years the firm held the monopoly of this trade in Paisley. With his success, he built himself a townhouse at Back Row, Ferguslie. He then, as a silent partner, funded the firm of Ross & Duncan at George Street, who had mastered the techniques of twisting silk yarn. On dissolving this partnership, James Coats built his first small mill at Ferguslie in 1826. In 1830, after perfecting his thread, he retired.

Kerr's nine-cord thread

His sons, James and Peter, founded the firm of J & P Coats. Soon, their brother, Thomas, joined the company. This family combination was ideal for a business undertaking. James had been a shawlmaker, Peter was an accountant, and Thomas an engineer.

The mill buildings at Ferguslie were largely increased in the 1840s. By this time, trade with America accounted for three-quarters of the firm's output, as another brother, Andrew, had built-up a marketing empire there. To counter the policy of home-trade protection, made by the Americans, the firm opened up in Pawtucket, Rhode Island between 1870 and 1883. Further mills were opened up in Russia, Germany, Austria, Hungary and Spain. In 1890, the company had a capital of nearly £6,000,000! It had, from small beginnings, become the largest undertaking of its kind in the world. In 1896, it absorbed the Clark empire.

Besides the Clarks and Coats, other threadmakers, such as the Kerrs and Carliles, had existed in the town, but, through time, were either absorbed by other companies or had failed in business.

THE RADICAL PERIOD

During the period between 1816 and 1820, Paisley became the scene of a 'Radical War'. It was a time of early trade

Paisley Thread Mills

unionism, political intrigue and reform, the reformers being the Radicals. The town at this period had seen mass demonstrations at Meikleriggs Moor, cavalry charges down the High Street, public riots and trials for treason. A provisional 'secret army', armed with radical clegs and pikes, was ready to overthrow the Government.

All this activity had been exacerbated by poverty in the working classes, high corn prices, unemployment and hatred of a Tory Government, who had little interest in the working man. An incident, in 1820, illustrates the conditions of the time:

'At 9pm, the Paisley insurgents had gathered at Maxwellton Hill. Daniel Bell led them to the houses of Robert Rowand of Millarston, George Muir, Craig of Lounsdale, some houses at Ferguslie and the West Toll. They, seeking arms, had collected four muskets and four fowling pieces. Further sorties to Foxbar and Leitchland brought more firearms, including some pistols.'

'At 11 am, the party arrived at Foxbar House, the property of Ross Robertson, and knocked on the door. Robertson peered out his bedroom window and saw about forty armed men. He asked them what was their business? They replied that they were soldiers of the provisional government and demanded arms and ammunition.'

'Robertson refused to co-operate and and argued that what they were doing was illegal. The Radicals said they would take them by force. Robertson woke up his son, and both fired guns on the insurgents from their upper windows. The Radicals returned fire. The story ended with one of the Radicals, Adam Cochrane, being shot dead. On hearing the approach of the Government cavalry, the Radicals dispersed.'

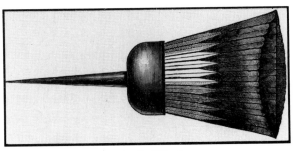

A Radical 'Cleg'

This episode is also mentioned in a letter written by John Parkhill to William Barr of Drums, dated 1833. Parkhill himself was a leading Paisley Radical. The parentheses are the present author's. The extracts are as follows:

'I beg to recapitulate briefly what I spoke of — the great reform meeting took place on the 17 July 1819 at which Neil, [Paisley representative to English Radical meetings] speechified, read and passed an address to the nation. On the 16 August, following the massacre at Manchester, a meeting on that subject was held on 11 September, both of which meetings were held on Meikleriggs Moor — it was, when coming from the meeting, that the flag was captured by Provost Jameson and it was on the 1 November that the great meeting was held at Johnstone. Mark, all this took place in the year 1819.'

'I am not certain whether it was a fortnight before or after the Johnstone meeting that Neil went to England. The secretary of the secret society informs me he [Neil] got in money either £3 or £4 for his journey.'

'When he came home, his report was that England was ready to a man. That in the Spring, 450,000 would take the field, that further communications would be made and that a signal would be given, such as stopping the mail etc. His time was occupied betwixt this and the 1 April in distributing pikes, soliciting people to join the Unions, and arm themselves.'

'In telling those of the country what numbers were united in town, and what vast numbers had joined in the country, Mr Cameron (Greenock Radical) mentions one plan he had of a revolution, namely that every county would rise and kill their MP. This was an often repeated plan.'

'When the first of April came — I have told you of his [Neil's] parcel of proclamations, of his notes of the provisional government, and of his thousands of cash to begin the war. Although in getting up the Foxbar expedition, he proposed that they should buy a penny ha'penny's worth of powder each — this was all their magazine. William Walker, John Kilpatrick, Thomas Morton, D Wylie and Cameron can speak on this.'

'John Rowand was one of the Foxbar men. Neil wanted him to attack the starching house of Messrs Fulton, but John refused and received a benediction of damns. He [Rowand] had one plan of a most alarming kind to rout the cavalry. It was just exactly what the farmers do to catch a stray colt — only to have a contrary effect. This was to get a penny-worth of peas, put them into a hat and rattle them in the horses faces! "By God" said he, "they will run like the Devil". You would almost say that there is as much of the daft man, as the spy in him.'

'On the Monday, 2 April, there was a bunch of idle weavers standing at David Paterson's door, he came up to us and damned us. What were we doing with our hands in our pockets? Go — arm — be ready. The man laughed and he went off damning their souls.'

These stirring, if difficult, times were later recalled in 1834 by Paisley's MP, Sir David K Sandford. He remarked that 'the West-end of Paisley gave the tone of politics to Europe' and that for Paisley to be adequately represented, there would have to be one member of Parliament for every weavers shop! Some bright Paisley weaver replied, 'Naw, we would be wantin' twa'.

CHARTISM

No reference to political reform or the struggle for freedom of speech can be mentioned without the name of the Rev Patrick Brewster. He was appointed minister of the second-charge at Paisley Abbey in 1818. In 1835, he caught the political fever of the times. After attending a public dinner in Glasgow to hear Feargus O'Connor MP, he was severely censured by the Church authorities. Although holding extreme Chartist views, Brewster was opposed to the use of force, preferring moral persuasion. He carried his political convictions into the pulpit and was accused by the Church authorities of 'irritating the poor against the rich' by his sermons. The General Assembly asked him to hand over the manuscripts of these 'corrupting works', but he refused. Instead, he fearlessly preached them again in the Abbey Church!

Brewster Statue Woodside

In 1842, he was charged with a libel by his Patron, the Marquis of Abercorn, for introducing secular and worldly politics into Sunday sermons and for representing the working classes as the subject of grinding tyranny! The libel ended by craving that Brewster be censured and punished by the Church. However, by 1843, the year of the Disruption, the greatest number of his opponents seceded from the Church of Scotland. The remaining members, wishing to be relieved of a toilsome matter, absolved Brewster from the charges.

Brewster's influence on the working classes inspired them to hold numerous meetings, where they adopted his philosophies and condemned the Church authorities. He paid dearly for his outspokenness. When the first-charge of the Abbey Church fell vacant, he was passed over. Brewster died in 1859, and his admirers erected a monument to him at Woodside.

Other champions of Chartism in Paisley were 'Wee' or 'Auld Cleirhead', Robert Cochran. His sobriquet reflected his powers of logic used in some of the great debates that took place during the Reform Period. He later became Provost. Bailie Henderson, a cutler by trade, had supplied the Radicals with weapons. He too became Provost. 'Citizen' Kennedy was a Methodist minister. His father, holding extreme political views, prefaced his son's name with 'Citizen', at his baptism. Kennedy was an eloquent, strong agitator and advocate of reform.

REFORM

The much welcomed Reform Act was passed in 1832, and Paisley could now elect its own MP. The town celebrated with processions through the streets. Dinners were held in the Tontine Inn, the toast of the day being 'The King, and may he never forget that he derives all his power from the people'.

The Burgh Reform Act of 1833, for the first time, put the Council elections in the hands of rate-payers. The only losers in Paisley were the magistrates, who had their annual salaries abolished. They were also shorn of some dignity. No longer could they parade to Church every Sunday preceded by the Town's Halberdiers. Their reserved seats at the High and Middle Churches were let out to the public.

PAISLEY TOWN 1845

The Second Statistical Account describes the town:

'In regard to size and population, Paisley ranks third in Scotland. Its houses and suburbs cover an area of 2½ square miles. Perhaps the most spacious street is George Street; but in point of elegance, none can equal Forbes Street [now Place] which is lately opened. The newtown built in 1779 now contains upwards of twenty regularly formed and closely built streets. Its appearance has been greatly improved by the giving way of several low thatched houses to neat substantial tenements. Of modern erections, Garthland Place may be pointed out as one of the most elegant rows of which any town in Scotland can boast.'

'Williamsburgh, a village or suburb to the East, contains barracks adequate to the accommodation of half-a-regiment of foot.'

'Charleston, including Lylesland and Dovesland, is inhabited chiefly by weavers, and contains, though most of it was built these last few years, a population of nearly 4000

Old Cross Steeple

14

St. Mirren's Wynd

shoulder-high and carried into town. By this time, they had armed themselves with iron railings and fencing stobs. The magistrates confronted them at Glen Lane, where a goodly number backed down while the remainder stoned the police. The rioting mob reached the Oakshaw Cholera Hospital, where they seized the Cholera van and carried it at the head of the procession. It eventually ended up broken into bits and was couped in the Canal Basin at the bottom of Storie Street. The mob then proceeded to break the windows of all of the town's medical practitioners. (It was a common belief that they were in league with the body-snatchers.)

When the rioters arrived at the Cross, they were confronted by the Militia with guns at the ready. No-one was killed and the main crowd broke up, but a small party returned to Oakshaw. They smashed the hospital windows and managed to get drunk in the process!

The fears of the rioters were allayed to some degree, when the local authorities issued handbills offering a reward of £50 for the capture of the body-snatchers. None was found. A system of watchmen to guard the common graveyard was also set up. A similar system had been in operation in Paisley in 1829, when a 'Society for the Protection of the Dead' had been formed. The members took turn to guard the town's church graveyards at night. They also hired out metal cages or mortsafes, to put over the graves of the newly buried.

This cholera epidemic claimed 446 lives. Cholera was to return in 1834, 1848, and 1854. This last epidemic was contained due to the improved sanitary conditions in the town

Paisley, in the 19th century, was described as 'the dirtiest town in Scotland.' Its existing infrastructure could not cope with the large numbers of immigrant workers pouring into town. Following on the heels of Highlanders from Argyll, came the Irish in 1841. They collected in the lowest, dampest, dirtiest parts of the town. Parts of the Sneddon were dubbed 'Wee Ireland'. Even Paisley's Chief Constable — a man noted for his Christian tolerance — stated 'the Irish are no more troublesome than the Highlanders'!

LATE VICTORIAN PAISLEY

Late Victorian Paisley was described by John Lochhead in his book *A Reach of the River*:

'The town was full of smoky grime and industrial vigour, drunken squalor, and puritanical religion.'

'Sundays brought a riot of competing church bells, for it was typical of the town that no single church claimed ascendency over any one group of worshippers.'

'Mud in winter and dust in summer competed with slumdom's smells. They were never far away. The River Cart, that had once teemed with salmon had become no better than a public sewer.'

'The Espedair, its tributary, poisoned a whole residential area with its stench. At Well Street, the odour of the Gas Works permeated the area.'

'Whisky shops abounded. Drunkenness walked hand-in-hand with poverty, while temperance societies and Bands of Hope fulminated against the evil.'

'Mornings and evenings, the streets were flooded with mill-girls hurrying to and from work dressed in petticoat, rough shoes and stockings, with a shawl over their head and bodice.'

'Working men wore a cloth cap, or battered hat, cheap

inhabitants.'

'Maxwellton, Ferguslie and Millarston form the Western suburbs of Paisley.'

'Paisley, upon the whole, may be considered as a healthy place of residence, notwithstanding the occasional visits of epidemical disease.'

CHOLERA RIOTS

The unmentionable disease was Cholera. Forewarned of its approach, the Town Council took business-like precautions against the spread of this disease.

A temporary Cholera Hospital was set-up in Hutcheson's Charity School at Oakshaw. Back court middens and dungsteads were speedily removed. Houses were scrubbed down with soap and the walls lime-washed. The small overcrowded houses, particularly common in the Sneddon area, were to have their 'ventilation secured'.

The first case, reported in February 1832, was predictably in New Sneddon Street. Significantly, he was a hawker. Within four days, nine people had died. Thirty new cases were reported weekly. Due to the large number of deaths, a common graveyard was opened at Paisley Moss, near the toll bar off Greenock Road.

At the height of the epidemic, the health authorities fumigated the town. Six large tubs, filled with a mixture of sulphuric acid and chloride of lime, mounted on barrows, were wheeled through the town. Meanwhile, at the Moss burial ground, two shovels and a small piece of cord, with an iron hook attached, were found abandoned. The public considered this clear proof that body-snatchers had been at work during the preceding night. These gruesome implements were displayed the following day, in a Blacklaw Lane shop-window in the town's Sneddon area. An angry mob then went to the Moss to find a number of empty coffins. One of these was mounted

Street improvements, 1873

well-worn coats and trousers, and a shirt, but no collar or tie.'

'Their housing consisted of usually one room; some had two or three, which opened off closes and stone stairs, some well scrubbed, others ill smelling. These tenements varied in height from 2-4 storeys. Their back doors contained privies, primitive and inadequate. Alongside this, was the wash-house and a yard where clothes might be dried.'

WATER SUPPLIES

In 1838, the town's first supply of piped water appeared, taken from Stanely Reservoir. Rowbank was opened in 1870. This alone was quite remarkable, as the town was still bankrupt!

Glenburn reservoir and Camphill were opened in 1879 and 1883 respectively. This abundance of water supplies to the town certainly helped in the fight against water borne diseases.

Between the years 1879 and 1892 major sewerage systems were built and the four major districts of the town were adequately drained.

Other improvements took place throughout the 1870s and 1880s. During this period St Mirren Street was built and the North side of the High Street widened and built upon from Churchhill to the Cross. At the same time, the town's three bridges were widened, in keeping with contemporary street improvements.

After 1892, with the passing of the Burgh Police Act, large numbers of three and four storey tenements began to appear in Paisley's streets. For example, Causeyside was widened to 70-feet and built upon, mainly on the east side. Upper middle class housing, built from about 1860 onwards, at Castlehead, and Glasgow and Renfrew Roads, was of the villa variety.

These were built mainly by 'corks' or manufacturers who had made good from the textile trade or ancillary industries.

Prominent families like the Coats, did not generally subscribe to these arrangements. Instead, they occupied more isolated mansions such as Ferguslie Park or Woodside House.

Token gestures had been made by the 'big' manufacturers to house the poorer classes. A good example was 7-19 Calside, built in 1870 when Sir Peter Coats, James Arthur, and William Holms became trustees for the erection of these artisan homes. Brown & Polson built houses for their workers at Falside Road, between 1911 and 1913.

In 1919, following the Housing Act, Paisley proceeded energetically with schemes to fill the gap in housing needs. This was done so effectively, that, by 1939, some 6500 houses were completed. Schemes like Whitehaugh, Gallowhill and Lochfield were established.

SECOND WORLD WAR

During 1939-1946, Paisley Harbour took on all the trappings of a busy seaport. Having substantial quays and facilities, it worked at full pressure during the 'Blitz' period. In June 1942, it berthed a 'record' 30 fully laden vessels. In the following month, the first American troops appeared in Paisley.

Another major function for the harbour was to keep the factories in the area well supplied with coal. New vessels were produced in the town's shipyards. One yard alone producing 31 ships!

In May 1941, the Luftwaffe dropped a landmine on Woodside First Aid Post, killing 92 people. Another two were

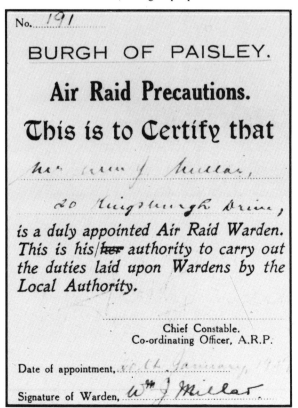

Air Raid Warden's Certificate, 1939

1946

foot of the Gleniffer Braes, Paisley became the largest Burgh in Scotland and began work on new housing schemes at Hunterhill, followed later by Glenburn and Foxbar.

Paisley has the distinction of being the first town to implement the Town & Country Planning Act (Scot) 1947, sometime after which the old George Street-Canal Street area was cleared and totally rebuilt. Similar schemes followed at Charleston, Glen Street, Mossvale, and Ferguslie.

The Paisley of the mid-50s was described as having 'a splendid site, heavy and light industries and a busy shopping centre, a busy little harbour, excellent parks, some noble buildings, a magnificent Abbey and a long history which it zealously guards.' A less vital town would have lost its identity to Glasgow long ago.

The inhabitants gather in coffee shops or pubs and there is a distinct atmosphere of the parish pump, where their talk is personal and local. They recognise everyone present. Strangers, known in the town as 'ootlanders', are not too unkindly observed.

Briefly, in the 1960s, Paisley became the highest exporting town per capita in Britain. By 1968, the River Cart was all but closed to river traffic, reflecting the fact that Paisley had never developed her river, as had Glasgow.

Between 1969 and 1971, the new municipal buildings were erected on the old Newtown lands between Cotton Street and Mill Street. At the same time, the fine old County Buildings were demolished to make way for the out-of-character shopping complex, the Piazza! and the River Cart covered over.

By 1975, Paisley was no longer a Burgh, but became the administrative centre of Renfrew District. A Festival of Paisley was held at this time, in honour of the old town. This included museum exhibitions, parades, and concerts. Paisley 'Bodies' had suddenly become aware that their identity and heritage could be lost.

It was this 'awareness' that prompted the author to found the Old Paisley Society in 1977. The Society 'keeps its eye on Paisley' as Disraeli directed, fostering civic awareness and a pride in the town's past. Cottages in the town's George Place were renovated by the Society and officially opened as the "Sma' Shot Cottages" in July 1985. The Weaver's Cottage in Shuttle Street opened officially in August 1990.

In 1988, this old immigrant/emigrant town held a 'large party' to celebrate its five hundred years as a Burgh. The celebrations were honoured by a visit from the Queen.

A VIP visitor, who came to Paisley, 'clothed in secrecy', was ex-President Ronald Reagan. He arrived at Castlehead Church on Sunday, 20 October 1991 and worshipped at this Church which had had connections with some of his Paisley forbears.

PAISLEY : A STATE OF MIND

The blood of the Paisley weavers still flows strongly today in the town's citizens. Paisley Shawls, carefully preserved in bottom drawers by the town's old ladies are treated with the respect of an old friend. They proudly boast that their forbears were Paisley Shawl Weavers.

'Paisley Pattern' carries the name of the town to all parts of the world. 'Paisley Tartan' has a bit of catching up to do! The town even boasts two Scottish country dances called after it - 'The Gleniffer Polka' and 'Paisley Mondays'!

Paisley is still Paisley; strangers to the town still strangers,

killed at Newton Street on the same night, by a second landmine. Another bomb fell on Havelock Terrace, killing one man who had decided to sleep through the blitz. Other bombs fell near Arkleston footbridge, and in Barshaw Park, with no casualties.

One Paisley-born 'Flying Ace' was Archie McKellar, DSO DFC and Bar. He, until recently, was a forgotten man. He is now recognised by military historians as being the most successful pilot in the Battle of Britain, having shot down more enemy aeroplanes than anyone else. As he died in November 1940, the day after the officially designated end of that Battle, he was not entered on the Roll of Honour as one of its participants. A recent monument to his memory was erected at Glasgow Airport, and a plaque has been placed at 4 Southpark Drive, Paisley, his birthplace.

Flight Sergeant John Hannah of Paisley, as an eighteen-year-old, won the VC in 1940. He hit the headlines because he was the youngest Scottish recipient of this medal at that time. In a RAF air-raid over Antwerp, his aeroplane had been hit by enemy fire. Due to his action in extinguishing the blaze raging inside the aircraft, the aeroplane successfully landed back home and its crew were saved. He died in 1947, aged 25, at Birstall, where a monument was erected to his memory.

POST-WAR PAISLEY

In 1946, with the extension of the town's boundaries to the

although even they have a club called the 'Ootlanders', which dared meet in the town!

"Whit Paisley dae A keep my eye oan hen?"

The 'Paisley Daily Express', known locally as the 'Wee Express' to distinguish it from the national 'Big Express', is read avidly in most Paisley households at home and abroad, for its 'hatches, matches and despatches'. The 'Wee Express' prides itself in giving a Paisley perspective on national events. There is an apocryphal story that said, when the Titanic sank, this newspaper carried the headline 'Paisley man lost at sea'!

It was said that when Paisley Buddies went on holiday — they took Paisley with them — they disliked spending their holiday with strangers! In this vein of provincialism, Paisley held an annual bowling competition called 'Paisley versus the World' at Millport. It was there that exiled Paisley Buddies played those from the town — the winners always being Paisley men!

The mills in Paisley were never 'dark Satanic Mills', but provided steady well-paid employment to thousands of mill girls. The girls, in a class of their own, even had their own native love call — 'I'll get ye!'

This native Paisley patois is still recalled by the town's citizens, when we learn that a 'Paisley knife' is a corkscrew 'Paisley mittens' the trouser pockets; a 'Paisley screw' a screwnail driven home with a hammer! An old Paisley toast, redolent of the day-to-day existence of a Paisley weaver's life is:

> Here's long life to you,
> Here's land rent free to you,
> Here's a child every year to you,
> And may you die in Paisley!

If you die in Paisley; the Paisley man has a choice greater than most. There is Paisley, Scotland; Paisley, Florida; Paisley, Oregon; Paisley, Melbourne; Paisley, Canada; and Little Paisley, New Zealand (now a cemetery anyway!) Should you wish to be buried at sea, then there is Paisley Seamount underneath the Mozambique Channel. If you are a member of the illustrious Coats family, you could be buried in Coats Land, Antarctica and be conveyed there by the Paisley built icebreaker the 'John Biscoe'.

END OF 'SPOOL'

Paisley's long history was not so much concerned in high affairs of state, although the town had its fair share of that in the earlier times. Paisley's history is more concerned with its Abbot and Abbey, its religions, witchcraft, trade riots, poetry and pirns, looms and shawls, bobbins and thread, and mill girls.

The people of Paisley matter first. It was due to these people that the town became the most successful and uniquely independent Burgh that Scotland has ever produced. It is a place still to 'keep your eye on'.

1) CATHCART PILLAR, PAISLEY ABBEY —
After Robert the Bruce died in 1329, according to
tradition, Sir Alan Cathcart VI, his old comrade in
arms, in the company of Sir James Douglas, in 1330,
sailed with the intention of taking King Robert's heart
to the Holy Land. Sir James Douglas was killed in
Spain when fighting against the Moors, but Sir Alan
Cathcart retrieved the heart and returned with it to be
buried at Melrose Abbey. This shield, bearing the
Arms of Sir Alan, was built into the South central pier
of the nave, then being rebuilt, during the later part of
the 14th century. According to tradition it was placed
there by Sir Alan Cathcart's son, to commemorate his
father's knightly, noble deed.

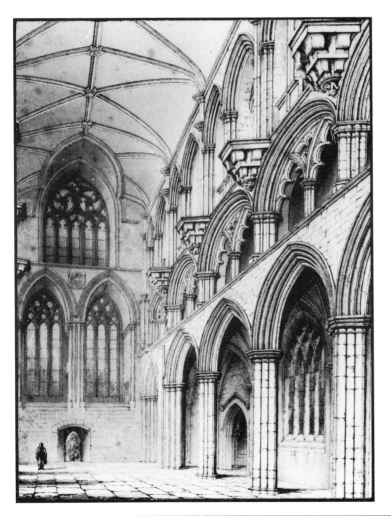

2) PAISLEY ABBEY NAVE c1850 —
The 13th century Great West doorway at
the rear leads to an aisled nave which is
distinguished by a main arcade unusually
graceful for its mid-15th century period.
It consists of a finely cusped triforium
above which is a peculiar clerestorey
passage breaking out round alternate piers
in corbelled projections. These corbels,
unique in Britain, are thought to be copied,
though less gracefully, from similar
corbels in Rouen Cathedral. The
grotesque carvings in their bases have
been attributed to a local sculptor Thomas
Hector, retained for his "skill and art" by
the abbey, between the years 1460 and
1502. The ceiling dates from the first
restoration in 1788 and was plaster painted
to resemble stone ribs.

3) ST MIRIN'S CHAPEL, PAISLEY ABBEY

c1850 — A curious barrel vault of independent construction occupies what had been part of the Abbey's South Transept. It was endowed in 1499 as a private altar by a local burgess, and its chaplain had quarters built above the main chapel. Underneath the window, a stone frieze depicting the life of St Mirin is seen, and may be based on the Saint's life as told in the Aberdeen Breviary first printed in 1510.

The effigy on the top of the altar tomb may be that of Princess Marjory Bruce, but its base, pieced together from fragments found in 1788, is now thought to have formed part of the Abbey pulpitum or choir screen built during the abbacy of John de Lithgow (1384-1433).

4) ALMSHOUSE, HIGH STREET

c1800 — The Wee Steeple, or Almshouse, was built in 1618, from stones taken from the ancient Chapel of St Roche, then ruinous, situated at the top of Castle Street. It was built to house and support six old, feeble men no longer capable of work. They were to be clad in ankle-length gowns and wear bonnets. In return, they had to offer up prayers, ring the bell on the steeple twice daily, keep the hospital clean, and cultivate flowers in the backyard. A more sombre duty was to ring the steeple bell, nicknamed 'Yammer Yowl', when a funeral passed by and to collect alms from the mourners. The arched passage, or pend, led to Oakshaw via Pen Brae. The buildings were removed in 1808, when Orr Square was laid off and a new passage formed to serve the Meeting House of the Baptists known as the 'Pen Folk'.

5) SLEZER'S VIEW OF PAISLEY IN 1693 — In the centre of the picture, viewed from Saucel Hill, rises Paisley's Tollbooth Steeple. To the right towering above the ancient village of Seedhill, the choirless remains of Paisley Abbey whose medieval nave now served as the only parish church in the town. The town's only bridge – the Brig of Paisley – first mentioned in 1490, rebuilt at the close of the sixteenth century, connecting the Abbey to Paisley Cross, clearly shows the old custom booth and port. The bridge was removed in 1783. Causeyside, running downhill left to right, consisted of single storey but-and-ben type cottages.

6) FIRST ABBEY BRIDGE SEEDHILL 1826 — Viewed from Seedhill, this first Abbey Bridge was built in 1763 to connect two established areas of the town built around Orchard Street and the Abbey Close. Both these areas began building in 1758. The bridge itself was of dressed stones. Beyond the right bank of the Cart stood the medieval nave of the Abbey surrounded by a huddle of little houses and workshops. The left-hand bank was occupied with the Town's Infirmary (built 1808). The two towers in the distance are the Tollbooth (centre) and the High Church.

7) ROBERT TANNAHILL (1774-1810) — Paisley's weaver poet born in Castle Street, son of a well-respected 'bien' weaver to whom Robert was apprenticed in 1786. Described by a contemporary as the 'prettiest shuttler' he had ever seen, Robert had a wee box on his loom where he kept his writings, and a slate hung on his loom-post for jotting down his ideas. At his cottage in Queen Street he composed. most of his best known songs. An admirer of Burns, he helped found The Burns Anniversary Society in 1805 in Paisley – the world's first Burns Club. In 1807, encouraged by friends, he published "The Soldier's Return" with poems and songs which made him famous. When a publisher declined a revised edition in 1810, and after a mental illness, the poet drowned himself in a culvert of the Candren Burn. The portrait shown was drawn one day after his death by another friend, John Morton. Tannahill's poems and songs are still popular today – 'Jessie the Flower o' Dunblane', 'Will ye go Lassie go', 'Thou Bonnie Woods o' Craigielee'. 'Are Ye Sleeping Maggie', 'Gloomy Winter'.

8) ALEXANDER WILSON (1776-1813) — Poet and ornithologist born in Paisley's Seedhill, where he became a weaver aged 13, and later a widely travelled pedlar or packman. He published his first poems in 1790. In 1792 his poem 'Watty and Meg' met with national success. A year later he was prosecuted and imprisoned for a libellous poem 'The Shark'. Published anonymously about the dishonest dealings of a Paisley mill owner. He left for America the next year where guided by William Bartram, a noted naturalist, he decided to devote himself to a scientific study of ornithology and in pursuit of which he made epic journeys mostly on foot across vast tracks of America. Wilson drew from life or from freshly killed specimens no less than three-hundred-and-twenty bird portraits, thirty-two of which were new to science. Later he prevailed upon the publisher of Rees Encyclopedia, where he worked, to undertake an American Ornithology. Wilson was to compile and obtain sufficient subscriptions for such an immense undertaking. After completion of the seventh volume, Wilson died. The eighth and ninth volumes were completed afterwards. Wilson died a famous man in Philadelphia but in relative poverty. He was elected a member of the American Philosophical Society in 1813 four months before his death, and was later to be known as 'The Father of American Ornithology'. His bronze statues stand in Cornell University and Paisley, but his best epitaph is from the singing birds that still bear his name – the Wilson plover, snipe, phalarope, petrel, warbler and thrush.

9) PAISLEY ABBEY FROM CAUSEYSIDE 1828 — An old Burgher Meeting house had been situated in front of Paisley Abbey. When it was demolished in 1828, this view looking over the river from Causeyside was opened up. The central figure wheels a dyer's barrow filled with yarn. A carrier's horse-drawn van emerges from St Mirren Street. A crowd of women are gathered outside the shop of bustling Betty Boyd, a fruit and vegetable dealer. On the right, talking to a man on horseback is John Hart, wearing knee breeches, with rig and fur white stockings, attended by his two greyhounds. He was a noted greyhound courser.

10) CHRISTIE BUILDINGS AND TERRACE 1833 — In 1827, James Christie, who had been a partner in a soapmaker's business in New Sneddon Street, purchased all the properties on the North side of High Street, between the Coffee Room and Paisley Bridge. He took down the houses that stood there and erected this range of three-storey buildings, which comprised eleven spacious shops, flatted houses, and warehousing, all of the first class. In the basement overlooking the Cart, he built a hostelry called Terrace Tavern. The whole speculative development was a financial failure for James Christie, so in 1833 the subjects were offered as a prize in a Tontine. If enough gentlemen subscribers could be procured to accumulate and invest a common fund, out of which they would receive an annuity which increased as other subscribers died, the last survivor would collect the prize. Needless to say, it did not work. Christie Street, built on the lands of Wester Crossflat, was called after this family.

11) ADVERTISING HANDBILL 1832—Duncan Henderson was a grocer and spirit dealer at No.6 Cowieston, Paisley (the south end of Maxwellton Street). He was one among many who by great effort induced others to grow 'Cobbetts Corn' in the Paisley district. William Cobbett, the famous political writer, came to Paisley in 1832 and astonished its inhabitants with his shrewd and good natured eloquence and was honoured with a dinner in the Saracens Head. At this time he visited the widow of Duncan Henderson and stated – 'on the same day when I expected to go and see Mr Duncan Henderson who, from his attachment to me or rather to my writings, had taken so much pains to cultivate my corn, I was informed that I had to see his widow. I went to see Mrs Henderson, at which she was very much pleased, and she showed me a letter written by me to her late husband in which she had set so much value as to have it framed and hung up as a picture.' Duncan Henderson had died on 17 October 1832 disappointed at not meeting his hero.

Cobbett's Dwarf Indian Seed Corn
FOR SALE.

As the time for committing the Seed of this highly valuable, most productive, and beautiful Plant to the Ground, is at hand, the Subscriber intimates, that he has a quantity of Cobbett's rearing, from his Farm at Barn Elm, Crop 1831. The Subscriber has also a part of his own Seed, grown last Year at Cowieston, from the Plants visited and so much admired by many thousands. From personal observations made by him, on examining various plots in Paisley and its neighbourhood, he has been led to conclude, that the latter end of April, or beginning of May, is the most proper time for planting the Seed in the West of Scotland. Correspondents in the Country are therefore requested to avail themselves of the present notice, by making an early application. The Subscriber has devoted his attention to the introduction of this Plant into Scotland, for the last three Years, under a firm conviction that its cultivation will be, from its highly nutritive qualities, very beneficial to all classes of the community. He recommends a light sandy soil, or fine loam ; the drills to be three feet asunder, and eight inches betwixt each seed ; to be set with plenty of horse, cow, or pig's dung, well rotted ; as the plants get up, to be well hoed betwixt the rows, and the earth drawn up to the roots—by paying attention to these simple directions, a fair crop may be anticipated. He had from 3 to 5 ears on each plant, so that some of them produced nine-hundred fold.

Ears 6d. each, or 4d. per ounce.

Cowieston, April 18, 1832.   DUNCAN HENDERSON.

Neilson & Hay, Printers.

12) PAISLEY SOAP WORK 1832 — The Sneddon bridge on the left was erected in 1792. The Common or Newtown Quay to the right, busy with horses and carts, could berth sloops of 40–50 tons, for up to this point the Cart was navigable. The large works was the property of William Sim & Co, hard and soft soap manufacturers, 4 West Croft Street (Abercorn Street). At this time there were only two other soapmakers in the town. These were John Bell, Smithhills, and Oliver Jamieson, New Sneddon Street. Commercial soap making had been introduced to the town by John Christie before 1764. As well as engaging in the Baltic timber trade, he was a founding partner in the Union Bank of Paisley (1788). By 1896, three large soapmakers had extensive businesses; The Gleniffer Soap Co, Lonend; Robin & Houston, New Sneddon Street (also candle makers); Isdale, McCallum, Caledonia Soap Works, Rowan Street. Ralph Isdale and John McCallum, both former employees of Robin & Houston, set up business in 1869. Their famous 'Thistle Soap' and 'A1 Soap Powder' became household names. John McCallum, known as 'Honest John', became MP for the Burgh in 1906.

13) PAISLEY ABBEY: NORTH SIDE c1835 — At this time, the only remains of the medieval Church were the nave and St Mirin's Chapel (seen at the rear). The crossing, North transept, and choir were largely destroyed when the central tower, nearing completion around 1550, fell. Over a period, the remaining stones were removed by locals and used as building materials. In 1730, the overhead belfry was erected. The old 15th century North porch, which originally contained a parvise, had an ugly, 18th century erection placed over it and was used as a session room. Although a crude restoration had taken place in 1788, Victorian vigour began the first true restoration of nave and transepts between the years 1859-62. Later restorations were to follow.

14) PAISLEY HIGH STREET c1835 — The tollbooth steeple, erected in 1757, stood at the corner of Moss Street and High Street. The elegant shops on the right side of the street comprised Williamson (china merchant), Boyd (shawl manufacturer), and David Brough (haberdasher). Outside this shop a lady is carrying an umbrella (first introduced to Paisley in 1788 by a Mr Weir). Next door was the Paisley Coffee Room, an elegant two storey pilastered building erected in 1809 – the favourite source of news and gossip for local businessmen. The town, whose population numbered 46,000, was well served with coaches. Lyon & Walker ran regular services to Glasgow, Edinburgh and Ayrshire. On the left of the street, D Dick (a bookseller publisher) had his shop. Beyond this, St Mirin's Wynd led off to the left.

15) PAISLEY CANAL 1839 — The Glasgow-Paisley-Ardrossan Canal was completed in 1810, but due to lack of funds only ran between Glasgow-Paisley-Johnstone. The view shows a fly-boat, pulled by a team of postilion horses, going under the bridge at King Street (now Saucel Street) at the end of which stood the Saucel Distillery (on right) and the Brewery of James Cheap & Co (left). The little buildings next to the canal were offices owned by the Canal Company. Beyond are the spires and chimneys of the town. In November 1810, at the Canal Basin (formerly Canal Street Goods Yard) eighty-five persons were drowned when a boat overturned while being boarded.

16) DR JAMES KERR 1769-1848 — This sculptured marble slab by Fillans was presented to Dr James Kerr at a public dinner held in his honour in 1840. Dr Kerr appears in the centre. Dr Kerr, surgeon, in association with Robert and James Thom, engineers, had been responsible for supplying Paisley with its first piped water. The first sluice was opened at Stanely Reservoir in July 1838, by Dr Kerr. When the water reached the town (specially decorated for the occasion), five new fountains threw up jets d'eau to the delight of the inhabitants. Church bells rang, triumphal arches were built, celebrations and processions took Place. Dr Kerr died in 1848 and is buried in Woodside Cemetery. Sadly, he is now a much forgotten man in Paisley.

17) PAISLEY 1840 — This view of Paisley looking south towards Oakshawhill is taken from the bottom of King Street, which passes underneath the railway bridge on the extreme right. A passenger train of the Glasgow-Paisley-Ayr railway (opened 1839) crosses over the bridge at the foot of Well Street. The old distillery situated in Well Street can be seen, just behind the steam engine's smoky funnel. The large factory building in the centre is the Underwood Cotton Spinning Mills. On Oakshaw ridge, populated with large merchant villas, the spire of the High Church reaches for the sky. The smaller spire to the left is of the old Tolbooth situated at Paisley Cross.

18) TEETOTAL TOWER c1840 — An eccentric lady, Mrs Caldwell began building this strange looking edifice off Renfrew Road in 1838. The pagoda styled tower was a beacon for the temperance movement for miles around. When it opened to the public in 1840 it became a great attraction as it housed a camera obscura. Admission was one penny. Visitors were treated to a lecture by 'Lady Caldwell' and served with lemonade and ginger beer by her, usually attired in a silk dress and using the heads of stockings drawn up over her arms as sleeves! George, her husband, would play a fiddle to those who wished to indulge in a penny reel. Incidentally, Mrs Caldwell sent her children to school, or to play, chained up to each other in case they became lost!

19) JOHN HENNING (1771-1851) — Born in Paisley, son of a talented carpenter builder, John became interested in wax modelling after visiting a travelling exhibition of wax busts just prior to 1799. Setting up business as a modeller in Glasgow and Edinburgh and building up his growing reputation he arrived in London in 1811. There he spent twelve years making restored miniature copies of the Elgin Marbles. Described by Josiah Wedgewood as a 'very ingenious modeller', he reached the height of his career when Princess Charlotte sat for him. Amongst other sitters were Sarah Siddons the actress and the Duke of Wellington. His friezes still adorn the Atheneum Club and the Royal College of Surgeons in London. He exhibited at the Royal Academy 1827-1829 and was admitted an honorary member of same in 1827. He received the freedom of Paisley in 1846, and died in poverty in London in 1851.

20) JAMES FILLANS SCULPTOR 1808-1852 — While an apprentice weaver in Paisley, young James astonished his workmates by producing, in his leisure hours, a wood carved model of an automaton weaver at work on a loom, powered by a real mouse turning a wooden wheel cage! He was dubbed as the 'mouse genius'! When, as a twenty year-old stonemason, he again astonished his colleagues with his facility in carving the capitals of the columns of the Glasgow Royal Exchange (Stirling's Library), he was dubbed 'The Young Athenian'. He became a professional sculptor and successively opened studios in Paisley, Glasgow, and London. In honour of his rising fame, Paisley honoured him with a public dinner in 1844. Leaving London in 1851, he returned to Glasgow and died there in 1852, leaving a large family unprovided. He is buried in Paisley (Woodside) under the figure, 'Rachel weeping for her Children', which he had designed for the grave of his father.

21) JOHN WILSON (1785-1854) — John Wilson became celebrated as 'Christopher North' through his writings to Blackwoods Magazine in Edinburgh. Described by his friends as a six-bottler, a sixteen stoner, an out-and-outer, a racer, an athlete, a poet, fierce-eating and good looking, and a damned good Tory! In 1820 he was appointed Professor of Moral Philosophy at Edinburgh University. In 1831, whilst attending a dinner in Paisley in honour of his old schoolmaster James Peddie, he was made an honorary Burgess of the town. Prior to this the Town Council had deliberated long and hard on the subject and had decreed that Wilson was ineligible – because he was an inveterate Tory! He is credited with coining the words 'Paisley Bodie' whilst addressing his fellow townsmen at another dinner in 1836 held in his honour; but if truth be known it was his Glasgow poet friend Thomas Campbell who suggested the idea! His statue stands in Princes Street Gardens today. A plaque marks his birthplace in Paisley High Street.

22) 'DAFT SANDY' 1805 — A lithographed drawing of 'Daft Sandy' was made in 1805 by Neilson, a local printer-publisher. Sandy lived in the Saucel area of the town. Not much is known about him other than he was a street beggar, who hung about the passengers departing and arriving by public coaches. With outstretched hand he would say 'I'm daft; man, gie's a bawbee.'

23) PAISLEY 'CORKS' OUTING TO GLENFIELD 29 MAY 1856 — These men were known in Paisley as 'Maisters' or 'Corks' – the town's leading businessmen. To celebrate the Queen's birthday they made a visit to the country estate of the Laird of Glenfield, William Fulton Esq (fifth from left). The chimney pot hats were particularly popular in Paisley as, it served as a receptacle for loose papers, samples of yarn or cloth. Some of the most interesting men were: left to right – fourth, William MacKean, Starch Manufacturer, later Provost; ninth – John Neilson, Printer; Seated centre – Matthew Tannahill (brother of poet) aged 77; Front row right – Robert Clark, Thread Manufacturer. Photograph taken by A Barr, a keen amateur-photographer (First Vice-President, Paisley Photographic Society 1858).

24) COATS FAMILY GROUP, 5 WILLIAM STREET 1856 — This family, to distinguish themselves from their illustrious relations Coats the thread manufacturers, called themselves the 'Petty-Coats'. Their business was as ham curers. William Coats, the father, sternly holding the family bible, joined his father, Jervis, in the ham curing business in 1821. Jervis's shop became known by customers as the place to palm off counterfeit farthings then circulating, as he had defective eyesight. To overcome this problem, the family had the counterfeit coins melted down and made into 'Coats farthings' and used as normal currency. The mother in the picture, Mary Wilson was the second wife to William. Joseph Coats, then a ten year old, is seated next to his father, became a student of Lord Lister and was the first Professor of Pathology at Glasgow University. George, his brother (back row centre), served for 60 years with W. & A. Coates, latterly as Chairman. Allan Coats (back row, far left) was the father of George Coats, the eminent eye surgeon, who gave his name to "Coats' Disease".

25) JAIL SQUARE 1857 — Prior to the opening of Gilmour Street Station in 1840, there were no cabs for hire in the streets. They had to be sent for. The County Buildings behind were completed in 1821. The Square was the place of public executions. In 1837 William Perry a Glasgow man and convicted murderer, was publicly hanged here. He was buried in the Jail yard but only after a phrenologist took a cast of his head! This early albumen photograph signed and dated by R Harris 1857 is very rare. Robert Harris, jeweller in Paisley and amateur photographer, was a founder member of the photographic section of Paisley Philosophical Institute. Its first meeting was held in 1858. Harris, a technical expert in wet plate collodion photography lectured them in the 'Honey Process' which allowed the plates to be kept in usable condition for nearly a week.

26) WEST FRONT – PAISLEY ABBEY c1857 — The classic lancet great west doorway once had a ramshackle lean-to building built over it. This was removed in 1788. The clerestory windows were infilled with stone to keep out the draughts, and 'keep the Church warm'. These were removed in 1862. The stone staircase built over the old cloister door which led to a large upper hall was finally demolished, in 1874. Just prior to demolition, David Semple, a noted local historian, claimed that this building showed no evidence of having been an early part of the monastery. Other authorities insisted that the buildings must remain, as they once formed the cloistral, dormitory wing of the old monastery.

27) NETHERCRAIGS BLEACHFIELD 1858 — Grass bleaching of linen yarn and cloth commenced around 1740 in the Nethercraigs-Glenfield area. The picture shows girls turning over the thread in the bleaching greens, while a man stands ready to scoop pure water, taken from an adjoining water channel, over it. The buildings behind contained washing houses, drying stores, sulphur and singeing houses, engineers shop and machinery. This bleachfield was owned by the Stirrat family and later by Coats, both thread manufacturers. In 1780, there were three riverside dyeworks in the town, and, with the supply of water from the Stanely reservoir to the town in 1838, this increased. By 1896, there were seventeen large dyeworks and bleachers throughout the town.

28) LITTLE PAISLEY, NEW ZEALAND 1849 — This is a view of Dunedin, New Zealand and Otago harbour, taken from the city's cemetery built in 1857. Little Paisley was removed when the cemetery was built. This little colony was first founded by John Barr, a former Paisley weaver. His family, and another five Paisley families, emigrated, sailing on the 'Philip Laing' and arrived at Otago harbour on 15 April 1848. Another John Barr, formerly of Barr & McNab, shipbuilders in Paisley, arrived in Otago harbour in 1852, but only settled in Dunedin some time later. Emigration to New Zealand was first discussed at the Paisley Canadian Society's meeting, held in 1840, at which New Zealand was put forward as an alternative to Canada. One member stated, 'little is known about New Zealand, except that everybody who went there was liable to be eaten by cannibals'!

29) BREDILAND HOUSE c1860 — This was the home of the Maxwells of Brediland, who had held lands in Renfrewshire from as early as 1487, and Brediland Estate since at least 1580. The family descend from the Maxwells of Pollok. In 1700 this house boasted ten feather beds, a going clock, a loom, and In the loft above seventeen loose floor boards! The family owned four horses, nine cows and one calf, and thirty sheep. Wealth indeed! The house was single storey rubble built, with swept attic dormers, crow stepped gables and thatched roof with a square stair tower, a possible later addition. The house was occupied until about 1960 and was eventually demolished in 1976.

30) DAVID STOW 1793-1864 — David Stow was born in Stow Street. A plaque in Causeyside Street records his birthplace. Leaving Paisley Grammar School with a classic education, Stow entered the world of counting-houses in Glasgow in 1811 where, appalled by the conditions of the poor children, he became a Sabbath School teacher in the Tron Church 'fishing' for pupils in the dangerous dark wynds of Glasgow. Stow determined that their education must be improved and opened his first school in the Drygate in 1826. It was innovative –it had a playground, unheard of for a city school! He published his book 'Teacher Training' in 1818 to great acclaim. By 1836 he opened his Normal School in Cowcaddens – the first teacher training school in Britain. His famous dictum 'Train up a child in the way he should go and, when he is old, he will not depart from it' is still valid today. He is commemorated by a bust at Jordanhill College of Education and Stow College, Glasgow is named after him.

31) THE RENFREWSHIRE TONTINE c1860 — This large bow front inn built between 1780-82, stood at Paisley's Newtown Cross. Over its principal portico was an antelope supporting the arms of the Marquis of Abercorn, its patron. The building had thirty fine rooms. Behind the bow front on the ground floor, was a coffee room with a grand geometry stair nearby leading to a large hall. In 1817 Edmund Kean, the celebrated actor, played 'Othello' here to packed houses. The popularity of this Inn was to last into late Victorian times, where Grand Balls, soirees and public dinners were held in the Abercorn Rooms. After the Town Hall opened in 1882, its popularity waned. Prior to 1969, just before it was finally demolished, the building held one last surprise. Below its cellars was unearthed a large stone cistern which reputedly dated from the old days of the nearby monastery.

32) CARLILE QUAY RIVER CART, 1864 — Paisley's first large, steam powered threadworks of James Carlile & Son, then at 13 Carlile Place, can be seen in the background. Carlile & Co claim to have been founded in 1752, but are first listed as thread manufacturers in 1784. The firm was absorbed in 1887 by J & P Coats. Carlile Quay (originally Slate Quay) was built around 1835, when it also received a handsome new crane. The picture, taken at low water, shows shallow draughted sailing vessels with one berthed in dock. This Quay sat near the junction of Wallace and New Sneddon Streets and was an important communication with nearby factories in the Sneddon area (left).

50 STORIE ST

33) PAISLEY BATHS 1868 — The first baths were opened at 50 Storie Street on 16 October 1868. They were erected by a private company and consisted of a large swimming pond (known later as the tuppeny pond) with various hot and cold water baths. The baths were handed over to Paisley Town Council who, by 1897, had erected two further ponds and hot and cold plunge baths. Needless to say, mixed bathing was not allowed! Demolished in October 1989, the site now forms a car park.

34) WILLIE LOVE (1818-1868) — Willie, a half-witted Paisley Worthy, was a humble pedlar. He could believe anything and was for years possessed with the idea that he bore an uncanny resemblance to the late Prince Albert. Under this delusion, he walked to Balmoral several times and once to London, hoping to be recognised by the Queen. Needless to say he did not get past the gates! A local squib publication had portrayed Willie as standing in a public place beside two known imbeciles in the town. He raised an action and appeared in Court dressed up by his agent, in the attire of a respectable intellectual gentleman, with strict instructions not to speak. The Sheriff, a stranger in town, and under the impression that Love really was such a gentleman, ruled that 'Mr Love should not be represented as on the same level as those deficient in intellect'. He won his case! In 1857, three pamphlets purporting to be an 'Autobiography of William Love' were published. Willie was proud of these and hawked them around the town, totally unaware of this clever burlesque. He regarded them as a serious history, and even sent copies to Queen Victoria, who graciously accepted them. Willie died in December 1868.

35) FOUNTAIN GARDENS 1868 — Paisley's first public park was opened in 1868 at a cost of £20,000. Its seven acre site was built on the former Hope Temple Gardens owned by John Love after whom Love Street was named. The view taken from this street shows the geometrical garden design executed by James Niven (former assistant to Sir Joseph Paxton). The magnificent cast-iron fountain, 30ft tall and 60ft in diameter, was the centre-piece. It was built by the Sun Foundry, Glasgow. The donor was Thomas Coats of Ferguslie, thread manufacturer. To maintain he local connection with Sir William Wallace, a seedling grown from the Elderslie Wallace oak was planted in the North-west corner of the Gardens.

36) ROWAN STREET – DOOSLAN STANE c1870 — Rowan Street began building around 1753. By 1815, it was completed as far as the Espedair Burn. The street was named after Robert Rowan, Laird of Dovesland and Kilncroft, its main developer (ancestor of the author). One old building of Dovesland (still surviving as a chip shop) can be seen on the extreme left of picture. At the corner of Rowan Street/Neilston Road can be seen Paisley's 'wee magic stone' the Dooslan Stane, a large whin boulder used as a rallying point, or soap-box, by the Charleston weavers, a radical lot in times of strife and trade disputes. The stone was moved across the road next to a public house (its namesake) and finally, in 1896, rolled to rest in the nearby Brodie Park, where it can still be seen.

37) LIBRARY AND MUSEUM 1871 — Scotland's first municipal museum, designed by John Honeyman, was opened in 1871. Peter Coats, partner in the large firm of threadmakers J & P Coats, was the donor. This, together with the considerable collections amassed by the Paisley Philosophical Society since 1808, made the venture possible. The building also housed a free library. In 1882, art and sculpture galleries were added, again paid for by Sir Peter Coats. The building was once more extended in 1901 and 1933 and included library extensions. New shawl galleries were added in 1974. In addition to its other major collections, the museum, naturally, has the finest collection of Paisley Shawls in the world.

38) HUNGRY JAMIE — In February 1870, Hungry Jamie, who had been drinking and boisterous in Moss Street, was taken to the Police Office. When placed at the bar of the Police court, he beseeched the magistrate to let him go this once, as, 'it was a long time since he had been there before and it would be a long time before he would be here again'. He was sentenced to thirty days imprisonment. In leaving the Court, Jamie said 'By Jove, this is a fine go. Here's the Puddock, the Juck and myself all in dumpy, and what will the town do without us?' Before November 1861 he had been in custody twenty-one times for breach of the peace and had a total of three-hundred-and-ninety-eight days imprisonment! Between 1862-1869, he was charged eight times with being drunk and incapable, with begging and malicious mischief, and had been a prisoner for one-hundred-and-twenty days. He had also been admonished and dismissed seven times. In 1872, he was charged with breach of the peace, but promising the magistrate that he would go to the Poorhouse, he was admonished and dismissed. He went to the Poorhouse and remained there until he died.

39) 'THE JUCK' – THOMAS DONALD — Thomas Donald was nicknamed the 'Duck' or 'Juck' due to having large feet and walking or waddling like a duck. He had been a pattern designer in Paisley's shawl trade, an occupation requiring great artistic skill. However, due to heavy whisky drinking, his clever mind became ruined and caused him to act in a foolish manner. To obtain money, he took to ticket writing, producing 'To Let' signs or posters for the local shopkeepers' windows. The colours he needed for this work were mixed up using sweet ale! All his money was spent on spirits and he died, at an early age, in the Town's Poorhouse on 24 August 1872. He is remembered in a little poem by William Brown:–

The Duck, who was more rogue than fool,
Was keen to make a sale of show-cards –
clever as a rule,
But, O, he liked strong ale.

40) GEORGE DOBIE Tobacco maker — William Dobie started producing brown tobacco rolls and snuff mainly for the local market in 1809. His nephew, George, expanded the business greatly during the first half of the nineteenth century. Dobie's production of 'Ringmaker' tobacco twists, snuff and candles during the second half of the century proved popular. By the early twentieth century, they had acquired the Glasgow firm of J & T Hodge and were producing cigarettes. In 1938, their new factory was built at Greenhill Road. The firm, by now famous for its Four Square tobacco products, bought businesses in London and Australia where production started in 1953. Due to production difficulties and low profits in 1955, the firm was bought out by Phillips & Co and closed. The 'Four Square' trademark meant good value and was not a reference to the four squares of the town.

41) JAMES J. LAMB, Architect 1817-1872 — Born in Paisley and educated at Paisley Grammar School, after which he joined his father's office, James J. Lamb typified the new breed of Victorian professional gentlemen. He was well-educated and had wide interests. He contributed to Ogilvie's 'Imperial Dictionary' in 1853, and to 'The Harp of Renfrewshire' in 1871. When the Artisans Institute opened in 1847, he was chief promoter of lectures aimed at improving the education of the working class. In 1858, he founded 'The Tannahill Club' and posthumously published an edition of Tannahill poems, in 1873. Many buildings were designed by him, including School of Design (1848), the Grammar School at Oakshaw (1863), and Municipal Buildings, Renfrew (1872).

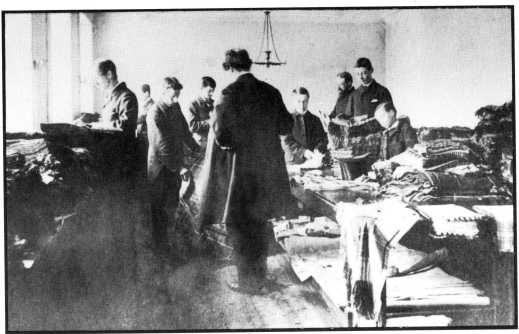

42) SAMPLE ROOM, SHAWL WAREHOUSE — The photograph illustrates a typical shawl manufacturers' sample room of the late 1870s. The sample room usually formed part of a larger warehouse and it would contain books filled with design drawings, cloth samples, and finished shawls, where prospective buyers would come and inspect the finished product. Two gentlemen in the picture are examining a tartan shawl in the premises of Daniel Murray Jnr & Co, shawl manufacturers. Tartan shawls appear everywhere. This Company, along with others in the town, had, in order to survive in the late 1870s, turned their hands to making tartan shawls, as the market for 'Paisley Shawls' had gone out of fashion.

43) DAUNIE WEIR – 'THE PAISLEY PERAMBULATOR' (1813-1879) — Daunie Weir was born in Charleston Village in 1813. He worked as a weaver until he was thirty. Giving up the loom, due to trade depression, he became a street pedlar of chapbooks and penny pamphlets. His favourite ballad, which he recited and sold in the street, to the great delight of local children, was 'Watty and Meg'. One Paisley citizen once asked Daunie if he had managed to rid himself of his hosts (fleas and lice). Pointing over to a church graveyard he replied that 'many people under the grass would be glad of them'! Once in Jail Square, he saw a preacher who had just finished his address to a large crowd. Considering himself a bit of an orator, he climbed on to the platform to preach. As his feet were bare, he stood upon his bonnet! He was then charged with breach of the peace. His fellow townsmen, out of sympathy, gave the Captain of the Police money for Daunie, which he was to receive on a rationed basis, from time to time. For a wager, when Daunie, known then as Paisley's 'Flying Stationer', was forty-three, he astonished everyone by walking barefoot, from the Canongate in Edinburgh to Paisley, in the space of fourteen-and-a-half hours, attaining a speed of $3\frac{1}{2}$ mph over a distance of 50 miles, and having called in at Bathgate and Glasgow for twenty minutes. All this was achieved on one glass of whisky, with a little bread and cheese. He had set a record only beaten years later by a Beith farmer. He died on 21 January 1879 after a short illness.

44) PLACE OF PAISLEY c1880 — After the reformation, the old monastery buildings became the property of Lord Claud Hamilton, nephew of Paisley's last Abbot. King James VI was entertained there in 1617 by the Abercorn family, descendants of Hamilton. By 1653, it was owned by Lord Dundonald, who made a 'nobill place' by alterations and additions in 1675. The Abercorns again became owners and, by 1760 several of the old rooms were being let out to sundry tenants. Gradually over the years, the class of tenant declined; the Place fell into disrepair and the old Abbot's kitchen became a pub. Notice the beer kegs and hand-cart, and the child in a three wheeled pram at the door. In 1904, the Abbey Kirk Session acquired the buildings and, by 1912, all the tenants had been removed and the buildings began being restored.

45) HIGH CHURCH 1880 — In June 1754, the High Church was opened for worship. By 1771, the steeple was finished. Both were designed by Bailie John Whyte. A great bell weighing almost 10 cwts was installed in 1776. The Town Council decreed that the Church could not ring 'the great bell' without their permission, this led to protracted litigation, which the Church won. The great bell lost its tongue and finally cracked in 1871. Near the Church, inset to whin causes is a 'pair of glasses' supposedly marking the spot where a mason working on the spire accidentally fell. In 1825, the 'Paisley Advertiser' published a spurious article claiming that there was a mystical little fairy-like figure called 'Wee Leach' who had climbed the steeple and sat on the spire smoking his pipe. The inhabitants of Paisley, abandoning shuttle and loom, came to see for themselves. Those blessed with good eyesight saw him; those deficient in sight did not, but soon acquired glasses of all shapes and sizes to see this little wonder! This may in some way account for the 'pair of glasses' put there by a prankster into the pavement!

46) TOWN HALL ST JAMES BRIDGE 1881 — The old bridge was photographed in 1881, just before it was to be remodelled and widened in 1882, the new bridge was called St James Bridge. The bridge is lined with people, and crossing it can be seen a horse-drawn goods wagon. The Town Hall buildings, appearing behind the bridge, were formally opened in 1882 thanks to the raising of fourteen thousand pounds by public subscription and a bequest of twenty thousand pounds by George A. Clark of New Jersey. The large Ionic styled building contained a suite of halls a grand organ, a splendid clock with chimes and carillion, smoking rooms and reading rooms. Behind the Town Hall can be seen the old steam-powered Abbey Mill.

47) ALEXANDER GARDNER 1821-1882 — One of the great photographers that Paisley produced. First became a silversmith jeweller and then later editor of the 'Glasgow Sentinel' newspaper. Gardner emigrated to America in 1856 to join, by invitation, the photographic firm of Matthew Brady. With Brady and others, Gardner was destined to photograph famous episodes of the American Civil War. Due to a dispute with Brady over copy-right and attribution of photographs, Gardner left to set up his own business, publishing in 1866 two volumes of captioned hand-mounted photographs called 'Gardner's Photographic Sketch Book of the War'. This was followed in 1867 by a photographic documentary of the construction of the Union pacific Railway His photographs of Abraham Lincoln, Gettysburg, Indians, Frontiersmen, and the Great Plains made him a true pioneer. He died in Washington DC in 1882.

48) CHURCHHILL/HIGH STREET c1883 — In order to build the Liberal Club and widen the High Street, these old buildings were doomed for demolition. The building with its gable covered in posters, was once the home of an Alexander Taylor, Surgeon, 87 High Street. Looking out of the window on the morning of 19 February 1788, he saw a man riding up New Street and recognised him as Robert Burns, poet, newly arrived from Glasgow. The poet was invited into the house. His visit was to last ten hours. He was introduced to the principal merchants of Paisley, some of whom Burns recalls were 'worth twenty-thousand pounds'. The house was subsequently owned by Mr Hart, Writer, until 1846. Robert Brown, who occupied it until 1856 (and became Provost in 1856) then moved to Underwood Park. Provost Brown considered it a high honour to have lived in the house once visited by Burns.

49) ST MIRREN FOOTBALL CLUB 1882-83 — St Mirren FC founded in 1876 first played under rugby club rules for one year. Its first ground was at Thistle Park, Greenhill (1877), followed by Shortroods (1878), Abingdon Park (1879-81), Thistle Park (1881-83), Westmarch (1883-84), Fullerton Park (1894-95), and St Mirren Park, Love Street (1895). In 1882-83 season, St Mirren first won the Renfrewshire Challenge Cup as seen in the photograph. The team's colours at this time were blue and red striped jerseys and stockings with white shorts. The team won this trophy again the next season after three replays. By 1890 St Mirren became founder members of the Scottish League.

50) WILLIE McALLISTER 'The Charleston Puddock' — Once a chimney sweep, Willie became lame, due to a bad fall while working at the Bishopton Inn. He earned a meagre living as a seller of spunks at Paisley Cross. His uncouth short figure, together with his staff and favourite dog, Jess, gave him a sad appearance. He subsisted on charity and had many visits to the Poorhouse and prison. On seventy-two occasions between 1869-79, he was apprehended as being drunk and incapable. For breach of the peace, he was convicted seventeen times, with a total confinement of five-hundred-and-eight days. He was a frequent visitor to the photographic studio of William Brown, then situated at 9 Gilmour Street. There he was allowed to make the tea, and would always take off his hat and say The Lord's Prayer. Sinking into final dissipation, he died in the Abbey Poorhouse on 31 June 1883.

51) PAISLEY WEAVERS 1883 — Two old weavers in their aprons, Ritchie and Cornell, stand beside a dismantled loom. The photograph, taken in 1883, marks the end of an epoch after which Paisley shawls virtually ceased to be made in the town. The weavers were a remarkable class of men – intelligent and observant, devoted to politics, strongly or widely radical, great talkers when gathered at the close-mouth or in public houses, guardians of the Church, reformers of the State, proud patrons of learning, but overall good fathers, good churchmen and good citizens.

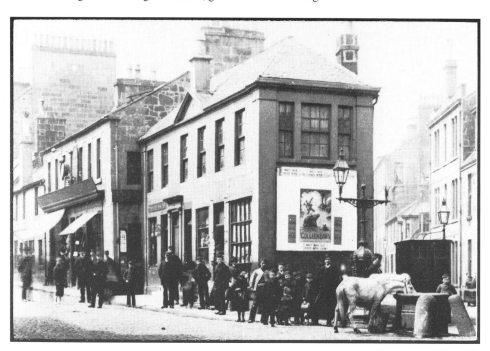

52) WEST END CROSS c1886 — Locally known as the 'Coffin End'. The building contained three ground floor shops and above a private reading room whose subscribers were mainly weavers. The large poster advertises Colleen Bawn, a music hall production which was appearing in Paisley Royalty Theatre. Behind the horse trough is a cast-iron 'pissoir'. These had been erected throughout the town in 1882. Some of the boys in the crowd are wearing woollen 'toorie bonnets'. Besides acting as a receptacle for all manner of things and a cudgel when folded, the 'toorie' was often burned like a firework after it had been daubed with a coating of damp gunpowder and set alight! This game was known in Paisley as a 'pea oye'.

53) GILMOUR STREET STATION 1888 — In 1878, Gilmour Street Station had been altered by the addition of more lines and arched bridges. Trains for these new lines opened to the public in 1888. This may account for the decorated buildings. Note the two hansom cabs waiting to be hired. The fenced enclosure formed part of the railway company's goods yard. Cowan & Co, whose horse drawn wagon can be seen, were railway agents and carting contractors for the North British Railway Company. This yard was to become the site of the Post Office. People are standing looking over the newly erected bridge parapet, which at this point surrounded a high level goods yard. Behind is a wooden signal box, and in the distance the spired gable of Holy Trinity Church can be seen.

54) LAST CANAL BOAT 1882 — A group of local business men, sitting in an old coal boat enjoy the last excursion in Paisley Canal's Basin. The old canal, which had opened in 1810 linking Glasgow, Paisley and Johnstone, was shortly to be drained and become the route for the Glasgow South Western Railway. With the opening up of Gilmour Street Station in 1840, the death knell of the canal was sounded. By 1843, the canal gave up both passenger and freight traffic in return for an annual payment from the Railway. Its horses and boats were sold off, leaving behind only a sound technology in making metal boats, which by 1838 had prepared the way for shipbuilding to commence on the River Cart.

55) QUEEN'S GOLDEN JUBILEE CELEBRATION 16 June 1887 — Thousands of people line both sides of St James Street to celebrate the Golden Jubilee of Queen Victoria's accession to the throne. The building to the left in St James Place (now Love Street) is decorated with flags and bunting. The Paisley Fire Brigade horses have been stopped to allow a photograph to be taken. Police constables line the route of the parade, to the rear of which can be seen various trade and society banners. The thatched roof buildings (on the near right) were soon to be demolished to make way for the Sheriff Court buildings (erected 1891). The town celebrations included a service in Paisley Abbey, dinner for one thousand children, a people's concert at the Town Hall, illuminations, and a display of fireworks.

56) GLEN CONCERT 1888 — Thousands of Victorians attended open air celebrations called 'The Glen Concerts'. These were held in the Fulton family estate called 'The Glen'. The concerts had first started in 1874 to celebrate the centenary of the birth of Robert Tannahill, Paisley's weaver poet. This particular concert, held on 2 June 1888, featured the Tannahill Choir, led by conductor J Roy-Fraser. The artist at his easel, preparing to paint 'The Glen Concert', is John Lavery, who had spent some time in Paisley painting portraits of his patrons, the Fulton family, and local landscapes. The concerts ceased to exist in 1935, but the funds raised at concerts between 1874 and 1884 built the statues of Robert Tannahill and Robert Burns in the town.

57) QUEEN VICTORIA'S VISIT ABBEY CLOSE 23 August 1888 — The occasion of the Queen's visit was to mark the fourth centenary of the Burgh of Paisley. The Queen appears seated in the carriage, underneath an umbrella. Provost Cochran standing in the street behind the carriage has just given her a civic address. A hundred picked men of the Argyll and Sutherland Volunteers form the guard of honour. Leading citizens of the time are placed on a platform built in the grounds of the Abbey (left). At the top left, the head of Tannahill's statue appears through the platform. Round the neck had been placed a garland of flowers. The Royal party consisted of Princess Beatrice, Princess Alice of Hesse, and the Grand Duke of Hesse.

58) ABERCORN FOOTBALL CLUB 1888-89 — Founded in 1877, Abercorn Football Club played at East-end Park near Bank Street, their first permanent ground. They later moved to Blackstoun, where they first won the double in season 1888-89. This event has been captured in the photograph – on the left is the Renfrewshire Challenge Cup and on the right, the Paisley Charity Cup. They repeated this performance the following season. In 1890, they were founder members of the Scottish League. In 1893, they played in the second division; dropping out of league football in 1915, through want of a permanent pitch. On occasions, they Played at Ralston Football Park at East Lane, now the site of a supermarket. The Club finally closed down in season 1920-21.

59) WILLIAMSBURGH – GLASGOW ROAD c1889 — Looking East along Glasgow Road is the weaving village of Williamsburgh. The single storey house to the right was the lodge house to Crossflat House, the grounds of which now encompass Paisley Grammar School. Outside this house can be seen the recruiting sergeant from the nearby Williamsburgh Barracks. The Paisley Tramway horse-drawn tram in the centre ran from its Hawkhead Road terminus to Thomas Street in the West-end. Williamsburgh was originally feued off by William Buchanan, Merchant, Old Sneddon Street, around 1781. It is probable that this village was called after him. The high wall of the Military Barracks can just be seen beyond the distant lamppost on the left.

60) LAIGH KIRK, NEW STREET 1890 — Built in 1738 it was the town's second church. Its second minister, Peter Scott appointed in 1740, was so poorly paid that one of his elders, Gavin Rowand, lent him a bed! Between 1756-1766, John Witherspoon was the minister. Leaving Paisley in 1768, he became principal of Princeton College and helped frame the American Declaration of Independence, of which he was a signatory in 1776. In January 1819 a great political Union meeting was held here by Paisley Radicals. In 1835, with the church in use as a hall, the famous Daniel O'Connell MP addressed a meeting there to maintain the political stamina of the Paisley reformers. In 1848 public meetings were addressed by the noted local reformers Brewster and Cochran, whose cry was 'Charter no surrender'. The old Church is now used as Paisley Arts Centre.

61) STREET VENDOR, GAUZE STREET c1890 — A street vendor is selling fruit and second-hand books from her barrows in Gauze Street. To her left is Abbey Close. Behind the elegant gas street light, the arched entrance of the George Temperance Hotel appears. Beyond the canopied shop-fronts further up, St James Bridge is seen. Behind the two barrows is the Newtown Dispensing Laboratory owned by Dr Hunter, surgeon and occulist. This four storey terraced building formed the corner between Gauze Street and Smithhills Street. Horse drawn tram lines can just be seen in Gauze Street. These were laid down in 1886. The Piazza, erected in 1971, now covers the site of these former buildings.

62) WILLIAM NOTMAN 1826-1891— Besides being a cowfeeder and a carrier of families, Notman's grandfather, as a Town Guard, took part in the last ever night-watch of Paisley Tolbooth Jail in 1806. When Notman's father failed in business in 1856, young William, by this time a keen amateur photographer, emigrated to Montreal where by 1858 he established his first studio. By the 1860s he had studios in Ottawa and Halifax, and by the mid 1870s a studio in the USA. By this time Notman was Canada's leading photographer. He recorded the growth of a young nation and was shrewd enough to pose Buffalo Bill alongside Chief Sitting Bull for a remarkable double portrait. The picture is of a commemorative Canadian postage stamp – not many Paisley men have been so honoured!

63) 'THE SHOWS', CLAYHOLES 1893 — On the 12 June 1888, the Town Council agreed to let the large piece of vacant ground at Caledonia Street for 'The Shows'. The area was known as the Clayholes, and, as its name implies, the site had been formerly used for the mining of clay, mainly used for brick-making. Previous to this time, the Shows had been held in County Square. The Show stalls have a wild West flavour. William Cody, better known as Buffalo Bill, made an appearance here, with his touring Wild West Show. Notice the two boys in the foreground playing at 'bools'. In the palmy days of the shawl trade, Paisley boys played with 'waft balls' made up from pirns of fine wool weft, made up of discarded 'ravellings' from the weavers' shop floor.

64) KELBURNE CRICKET CLUB c1895 — The Club was founded in 1860, first playing at grounds in Blackhall. In the early days, it was one of the foremost clubs in Scotland, their rivals being at that time the Paisley Thistle (instituted 1851). The Club moved to Whitehaugh in 1900. Around the 1930s, Willie Nichol arrived in Paisley on his transfer from Sunderland to St Mirren FC, and established himself over the following decades, as, arguably, the greatest all-round cricketer in the Western Union. He is best remembered for his brilliant score of 93 against Yorkshire at Hamilton Crescent, and his legendary dismissal of Bradman at Mannofield in 1953. 1951 was the Club's 'anno mirabilis' when they lifted the Western Union Championship in the final beating their arch-rivals Ferguslie at Meikleriggs, and in the same season won the McCulloch mid-week League.

65) JOHN SHANKS 1827-1895 — Born in Paisley. In 1851, Shanks advertised himself, to the Paisley public as 'plumber and gasfitter', 32 High Street, 'where from steadiness and attention to all orders and moderation in charges, he hoped to merit a share of public patronage'. After a few years, the business moved to Barrhead and, by 1864, he took out his first patent for his No.4 flushing WC, which was tested by Shanks himself by throwing his nearest apprentice's cap down the pan and flushing it away – Shanks shouting excitedly 'it works!' Between 1862 and 1895 Shanks took out over sixty patents and founded his Tubal Works in 1866. Little did he realise that from his modest beginnings in Paisley, the name of Shanks would become 'the best known household name in the world' and become, in West of Scotland patois, the 'Shanky' or 'Shunky'.

66) FERGUSLIE CRICKET CLUB c1894 — Ferguslie Works Cricket Club was founded in 1857. As Ferguslie Cricket Club, they had their first game against Kelburne Cricket Club on a field at Millarston in May 1887. It remained at Millarston for two seasons. In 1899, J & P Coats opened up Meikleriggs as a recreation ground and the Club was invited to set wicket there. Initially membership was confined to employees of the threadworks. It quickly became established as one of the largest Clubs in the West of Scotland and formed part of the Western Union, whose championship it won many times. Other trophies won included the Rowan Cup, McKenna Cup, Express Cup, and McCulloch Cup. In recent years local support and finances ensured that, when under threat of falling to developers, the present ground was saved. The Club celebrated its centenary in 1987.

67) WELLMEADOW c1895 — The East-end of Wellmeadow Street was feued off for building in 1777, and the West-end in 1761. This suburb originally consisted of small weavers cottages, but by the 1880s, larger, three storey tenements replaced some of them. The mixture of old and new can be seen in the picture. Well Street, to the left, originally Lonewells, was the old thoroughfare that led to Blackston Estate. The central tower in the background belonged to the first, purpose built, Sabbath School erected in Paisley in 1873. The land belonged to Oakshaw West Church and the new building was funded by William Clark of Newark, New Jersey, thread manufacturer, in memory of his wife Maggie Symington. Notice the number of horses and carts in this busy street.

68) UNVEILING BURNS STATUE, FOUNTAIN GARDENS On 26 September 1896, Lord Rosebery unveiled the Burns statue in the Fountain Gardens. The proceedings began with the Tannahill Choir singing Burns' songs, accompanied by the Ferguslie Brass and Reed Band. After much discussion by the Town Council, of where to site this fine statue by Pomeroy, the Fountain Gardens were finally chosen. Funding for the statue had been first mooted in 1883, by a number of gentlemen in the town. The Tannahill Choir agreed to 'sing up' funds for its erection and the first concert took place in 1884 at 'Craigencore'. From that time onward concerts were held in The Glen.

69) TWO WRIGHTS c1897 — This rare studio photograph by Pearlmann & Co., Photographers, Causeyside Street, shows two wrights in their working clothes. The younger man is wearing an apron and holds a folding rule in his hand. Seated, his colleague holds a spirit level. Notice the heavy well-worn boots, the baggy turned-up trousers, and the waistband of the older man. In 1723, when the town's population was only three thousand, the wrights mustered enough courage to form themselves into a society. Their motto was 'Join, all in one'. Their trade was strictly regulated – no journeyman shall work in the town without knowledge of their masters – no master shall lend or borrow tools from any tradesman who was not a member.

70) LADY LANE FLOOD 11 AUGUST 1897 — This flood which delighted the 'weans' of Lady Lane was caused by the St Mirin burn overflowing. Lady Lane was known as the Vennel in old Abbey charters, and connected Wellmeadow to Longait (Canal Street). It was called Lady Lane after the Lady Priest's House which once sat there (first mentioned in 1488). The Lady Lane Monumental Works (extreme right) belonged to William Currie and the four storey tenement behind was completed in 1891, to designs by Peter Caldwell. Behind the wall at the bottom of the Street, stood the town house of Peter Coats (thread manufacturer), demolished to make way for the Regal Cinema, built in 1930. Argyle Street (1884) can be seen on the left.

71) EMPIRE MUSIC HALL, MOSS STREET 1898 — In 1896, the old Assembly Rooms in Moss Street became the Royal Empire Music Hall. In 1898 the theatre was reopened as the Empire Music Hall. This is the occasion for the photograph. Colourful characters who ran the theatre were Dalno Fritz and his wife, both German. She collected the money at the pit stalls; he stood at the entrance wearing a tall hat, white scarf, and white gloves, shouting 'all pit and stalls this way'! Occasionally he would appear on stage as a sword swallower (his former occupation) and announce to the audience that he had not done this for some time. As it was a hefty sword, his act usually brought the house down! The theatre closed in 1906 and became a billiard saloon until 1936. It then became a tearoom until 1977 and is now a Chinese restaurant.

72) McDOUGAL BROS OF MOSS STREET 1898 — This bookshop was opened in 1865 by John and James McDougal. The family, specialists in manufacturing stationery and bookselling, had by the 1890s additional premises in Causeyside and the High Street. James A McDougal, the bowler hatted gentleman, is the younger of the founder brothers. He stands beside his sister Anna. On the left, wearing a traditional long black shopman's apron is Matthew Gardner, whom Anna married. The shop front featured a large advertising thermometer, while the inside was best described as 'Dickensian'. This shop was given a new frontage in the 1920s. By 1978, the shop had moved further down Moss Street and is now known as 'The Paisley Book Shop.'

73) NEW STREET 18 March 1899 — A new street 21-feet in width was built in 1734 to connect High Street with Causeyside. When the picture was taken, the cobbled street was just as narrow. The two storey building on the right with its small projecting sign advertises J McFarlane, bird dealer (keeping caged linnets had been very popular with the old weavers). The gap in the buildings further up, led to the stable-yard of the Bull Inn Posting Establishment at 5 New Street, owned by Charles Stevenson. In addition to running an inn, he hired out horses, dog carts, saddles, post horses and funeral hearses. On the left side, the sign of 'Pinkerton, Ham Curer', an old family business is seen. At the top of the street is Ballantyne's bookshop known as the 'Pen Corner'. Beyond is Churchill and the High Church.

74) THE BOHEMIAN CLUB 1890s — In 1895 The Bohemian Club was founded and its first chairman was John J Todd (back row, extreme right). The objects of the Club were:– the consideration and discussion of subjects of general interest to its members; the reading and criticism of essays and the discussion of works of literature. The Club, started in this humble way, soon established itself. When the Club reached its Jubilee John J Todd was again invited to take the chairmanship. The Club's transactions are not publicised, although full minutes are kept. It is well known, however, that besides holding ordinary debates and an annual dinner, the members entertain themselves histrionically and musically. Jack House, the Glasgow author, described the Club as the only one of its type in Scotland, unique!

75) PAISLEY FLORIST SOCIETY VISIT TO TOWN'S GREENHOUSES c1900 — Paisley Florist Society is the oldest in Scotland. From its foundation in 1782, its members, mostly handloom weavers, specialised in growing auriculas, carnations and pinks. The laced pink had a particular appeal, since it complemented the exquisite delicate designs then being produced in the town's looms. In 1813, a silver-topped snuff mill was presented to one Archibald Duncan, for the twelve best pinks reared. A second prize was awarded to James Findlayson, Florist, Seedhills, Paisley. In 1806 James Findlayson, who since 1794, had been exhibiting pinks in Paisley, sent some to the USA. The recipient was Alexander Wilson (the exiled Paisley ornithologist), who wrote back that the flowers 'were greatly admired by our American florists'.

76) CANAL RAILWAY STATION, CAUSEYSIDE c1900 — Canal Station, with its elaborate ornamental wood construction, belonged to The Glasgow and South Western Railway, who opened this line in 1885 over the route of the old canal. The Station was eventually closed in 1983. Beyond the horse drawn waggon in the distance is the old Corse House, situated between Neilston Road and Calside. This two storey house, with attic, was the one-time property of Bailie John Smith. It was recorded in Semple's 1787 map of Paisley, and was considered one of the best residences in Paisley at that time. The house had been built on the old medieval lands of Muyraes Malyng, where once stood St Ninian's Cross.

77) MUSEUM BAR c1900 — The Museum Bar was set up in Gauze Street by a Peter Lees. Its big attraction was inside, where glass-cased curios fought for space with large stuffed animals, all on display. The owner by this time a James McLay, Wine and Spirit Merchant, had arranged to have them removed prior to the demolition of the building. The site had been bought by the Methodist Church and their building, the Central Halls, opened in 1908 still occupies the site.

78) QUEEN'S OWN YEOMANRY CAMP AT DONALDS' WOOD 1900 — This regiment then resident in Paisley had set up a camp at Donalds' Wood prior to their departure to the South African War. Their arrival had caused a wave of excitement and patriotism in the town and they were honoured, together with local volunteers, with a public reception on 17 January 1900. The soldiers are riding up Gleniffer Road to the camp. Stanely Reservoir is on the right, and beyond the camp is the Paisley-Barrhead Caledonian Railway built in 1898 with stations at Stanely and Glenfield. The site of the camp until recently was occupied by St Aelred's High School.

79) INDUSTRIAL SCHOOL, ALBION STREET c. 1900 — This large polychrome brick building, approached from Albion Street (right), was a school for neglected children. It opened in 1870 and had accommodation for one-hundred-and-twenty-six boys and fifty girls. They were instructed in reading, writing, arithmetic, and various trades. Further additions were built in 1896. These comprised a new dining room, gymnasium, swimming bath, and additional industrial workshops. The playground shows a crowd of pupils enjoying a game of football. The site is now occupied by Council houses in Albion Street with St Mirren Park football ground beyond the wall to the left.

80) GILMOUR STREET 1901 — The opening of a street, leading from the old County Buildings (rear of picture) to connect with the Cross and to be called Gilmour Street, was first mooted by the Town Council in 1816. The School of Design with its symmetrical facade had been opened in 1848. Initially funded by the Government, it was aimed at educating the artisan designers of the town in art and science. Here they studied 'Fine Art' and the workings of machinery to acquire 'taste, which could be applied with profit to the town's manufactured products. James Elder Christie and William Kennedy, both painters, studied here. The School of Art was bought by the Town Council in 1885 to form offices. In 1970, the whole range of buildings were demolished to form the Piazza.

81) ARROL JOHNSTON: FOUR SEAT DOG CART 1901 — Between the years 1901 and 1913 Arrol Johnston motor cars were made in Paisley, in the former factory of the Underwood Spinning Mills. There the Company also made special snow 'tractors' for Shackleton's 1908 Antarctic expedition. From 1919-1932, William Beardmore made 'buses and taxis in this same factory. John Ridley of George Place, Paisley also built the 'Ridley', as a 6-hp two-seater car or van from 1901-1907. Only about twelve were built, as the Ridley Autocar Company later moved to Coventry. Another Paisley-built car was the Seetstu made by James McGeoch & Company at 11 Incle Street, from 1906-1907. It was a small, 3-hp, two-stroke engined affair of which only about six or seven were built.

82) JOHN NEILSON INSTITUTION 1902 — John Neilson of Nethercommon (1778-1839) had been a successful grocer in his native town. In 1839, before he died, he set up a trust deed to build and endow a school. By 1852 a school had been built on the site of a bowling green, to the design of Charles Wilson. To gain entry, boy pupils had to have lived in Paisley for three years and their parents had to be poor or dead. Some of the school rules issued to pupils on the opening day were as follows:– Pupils are not allowed to carry lucifer matches, gunpowder, or firearms. Pupils are strictly prohibited from the use of tobacco! The school gained, in 1900, a gold medal at the Paris Exhibition for its educational exhibit. By 1968 the school had outgrown its premises and moved to a new site at Millarston. By 1978, 'The Parritch Bowl' was closed down but has now been converted for private residential use.

83) HAY WEIGHS INN, KING STREET c 1902 — About 1794, John Gibb and Nisbet Sinclair, both innkeepers, erected a hay-weighing machine in King Street. The Hay Weighs Inn became established on this site. This old hostelry appears on the left side of the street [with its wide close and projecting sign]. Outside, three horseless hansom cabs await hiring. Beyond the little single storey cottage, originally built by Robert Rowan, is the old lane continuation of Sandholes, which led past John Street and thence to Woodside House. The two storey building beyond the lane was once owned by Dr J S Picken. The railings to the right belonged to the Free Martyrs Church (now Martyrs Parish). This Church was built in 1847. The ground originally belonged to the Rowand family, who sold it to the Church.

84) CATTLE MARKET, ST JAMES STREET c1902 — Cattle markets were held in May and August at fairs. St James Fair was first held in 1661, in what is now called St James Street. This market, which used to extend over three days, included a horse race at which the prize of the Paisley Silver Bells was awarded. At the bottom of St James Street stands Holy Trinity Episcopal Church, erected in 1833. The Sheriff Court and County Buildings on the left, completed in 1891, form the corner with Love Street. Glen Lane, formerly Glen's Lone, appears to the left.

85) CAUSEYSIDE STREET 1903 — It was proposed by the Town Council, in 1900, to widen Causeyside Street to 70ft. The narrow lane, on the right led to Paton's Espedair Works which was well-known for making packing cases and tins of all shapes and sizes particularly for the food trade. J & M Swan's horse-drawn delivery van sits outside their bakery shop. Beyond the 'gas light' stands a hansom cab. Downhill a man is riding a large trace horse, then a common sight in Causeyside Street. Due to its steep slope, trace horses were employed to haul up heavy loads. The barrier in the middle of the street indicates that the work of regrading the troublesome slope was just about completed.

86) GLEN HOUSE, GLENFIELD 1903 — Around 1859, William Fulton, Laird of Glenfield, built this mansionhouse. The Fulton family had made their wealth through bleaching. Their Dyeing and Finishing Works nearby became one of the largest and best equipped in Britain. It was here that 'Glenfield Starch' was first made, a product which became a household name. Besides being patrons of the Glen Concerts held on their estate, the Fultons were collectors of fine paintings. The family left the paintings to the town, as part of the Fulton Bequest in 1933. The house is now demolished, but the garden in the photograph, much changed, can still be seen as part of a public park today.

87) COUNTY SQUARE c1903 — To provide Paisley cabbies with a retreat where non-alcoholic drinks were available, Mrs Jane Arthur of Barshaw donated the Cabmans' Rest. It was placed in County Square on 11 September 1877. Cabbies were noted at that time for 'nipping in for a quick one', between customer calls. It was hoped this gift would improve matters. A horse drawn omnibus, advertising Lipton teas, together with hansom cabs fill the square, awaiting passengers from the railway station. The elegant lamppost (right) had the date 1897 cast into the curved lamp bracket commemorated Queen Victoria's Golden Jubilee. These electric lights were erected throughout the town centre.

88) JESSIE ROWAT (1864-1948) c1905 — Jessie's grandfather Robert was a prosperous thibet shawl maker in Paisley - a burly man noted for stomping down Causeyside Street, taking up the whole width of the pavement to the terror of small boys. Her father successfully-continued the business with her uncles. Jessie grew up, in Paisley, in a world of colours, textures and designs. She married Fra Newbery, head of the Glasgow School of Art, in 1889. He was deeply involved with the work of Charles Rennie Mackintosh. The photograph shows Jessie dressed in a completely personal style. She wears a wool cape over a 'Carpaccio' dress with her own embroidered decoration. Her 'robe de style' was outside contemporary fashions and, as such, she was able to wear it for many years. In 1894, she established an embroidery department at the Glasgow School of Art, her influence bringing it international recognition. She is now recognised in her own right as one of 'The Glasgow Girls'.

89) WILLIAM SHARP (FIONA MACLEOD) 1855-1905

— Born at 4 Garthland Place, Paisley, into a family of muslin manufacturers and settling eventually in London in 1879, where through Sir Joseph Noel Paton, a former pattern designer in the family firm in Paisley, he was introduced to the artistic and literary avante-garde circles of the day – the Pre-Raphaelites. His literary career now flourished. in 1884 he published "Earth's Voices", followed by "Sonnets of this Century" which sold thirty thousand copies. Midway through his career, under the pseudonym Fiona MacLeod – which the author never would acknowledge in public – he led the revival in neo-Celtic literature with remarkable tales and romances such as "Pharais", "The Sin Eater" (1895) and "The Immortal Hour" (1900).

90) ROYAL ALEXANDRA INFIRMARY c1905 — As the old hospital at Bridge Street had fallen behind the times it was decided to build a new hospital. The foundation stone of the new hospital was laid by Mrs Stewart Clark on 15 May 1897. Funding for the hospital was given mainly through the largesse of the Coats and Clark families. The architect, T G Abercrombie, devoted days and nights to attend to all the complicated details, including fire-proofing the building. On 4 May 1900 the first patients were installed in this 141-bed hospital complex. Note the horse-drawn ambulance in the picture and the bust of William B Barbour, MP for the Burgh from 1885-1891. The site for the hospital was called Barbour Park in his honour.

91) **PAISLEY CROSS** c1905 — The range of buildings to the right between Moss Street and Gilmour Street were demolished in 1906, as part of town improvements. This was largely brought about by the liberal funding of Mrs John Polson of Westmount. The Square so formed – and now the site of the War Memorial – was dubbed 'Polson Square by the locals. The elegant buildings at the corner of Moss Street, with the clock above, were built by the City of Glasgow Bank after the old Tolbooth, then in a dangerous condition, was demolished in 1870. The balustraded corner building (left) built in 1875, now a Building Society, formed part of the new line of buildings fronting a new St Mirren Street. Work in forming this new street began in 1871 and was completed in 1877. Notice the open top 'sparkie' tramcar in the High Street, operated by the Paisley District Tramway Company, whose first electric trams appeared at Paisley Cross in 1904.

92) **BRODIE PARK, 1906** — This spacious park was donated to the town by Robert Brodie of Carriagehill (1807-1871), who had been a successful banker in the town. The park was opened in 1877 by Provost Murray. To lay off the park, trees were planted around the perimeter and alongside the carriageways. Ornamental drinking fountains, park benches and floral display beds were also provided. The park-keeper's house, left of the gates, also had a ladies waiting room adjoining it. The bandstand in the background was erected from funds raised at Tannahill Concerts in The Glen. In February 1885, two kangaroos presented to the town by the Marquis of Bute, arrived at Brodie Park, where a small house had been built for them. Sadly, both animals died within a month of their arrival!

93) PAISLEY GRAMMAR SCHOOL AND WM B BARBOUR ACADEMY c1906 — Through the influence of the Rev. P. Adamson, Paisley Abbey's first Protestant minister, 'The Grammar Scuil' was founded by Royal Charter in 1576. That it derives from a Pre-Reformation 'Sang Scule' attached to the Abbey is not certain. In 1586, the first building was erected on the South side of the School Wynd. In 1753, the school was enlarged on this site. In 1802, the third school was built on a new site at the top of Churchhill. In 1864, adjoining the existing school, a large school was opened to be called Paisley Grammar School and Academy. In 1898, on the lands of Crossflat House, the school known as 'The Paisley Grammar and Wm B Barbour Academy' was opened. By 1943, the school was badly damaged by fire. In the 1960s, the school buildings expanded to their present form.

94) PAISLEY HIGH STREET c1906 — Stead & Simpson's shop at 91 High Street on the left displays its boots and shoes to passersby, while further down, two ornate lampposts stand outside the entrance to the Globe Temperance Hotel. The building to the extreme right was demolished to make way for Paisley YMCA headquarters built in 1908. The old crow stepped twin gable house projecting into the street was built by Master Andro Knox, shortly after 1593. He was the minister at Paisley Abbey. It was reputed to be one of the oldest houses in Paisley. When it was erected, the minister put a window on its West side which overlooked his neighbour's property' and built a water spout to discharge rainwater on to this same neighbour's property! Needless to say, his neighbour, John Maxwell of Stanely, was not too pleased!

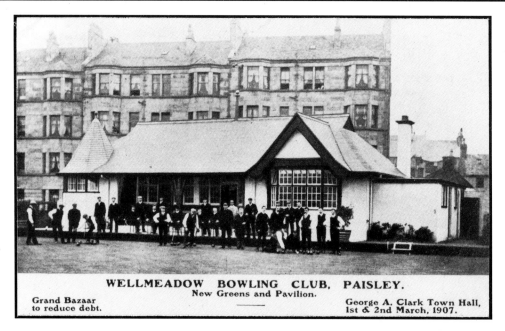

WELLMEADOW BOWLING CLUB, PAISLEY.
New Greens and Pavilion.

Grand Bazaar
to reduce debt.

George A. Clark Town Hall,
1st & 2nd March, 1907.

95) WELLMEADOW BOWLING CLUB, PAISLEY 1907 — This bowling club, whose members were part of Paisley United Bowlers Club (founded in 1849) then played at the Victoria Green in Lady Lane. The owner of the Victoria green was an Alexander Bowie who advertised in the local press 'the fee for a game shall be twopence; for a seat and perusal of newspapers, one penny'. In 1854 the Wellmeadow Club was established, eventually settling at Walker Street, and during the years 1905-6 purchased their original green, added some more, and built a splendid pavilion. By 1907 the Club had financial difficulties so a Grand Bazaar was held in the Town Hall that year to help defray debts. It was only in 1936 that the debts were cleared.

· ST GEORGE'S U·F· CHURCH : PAISLEY ·
· View From Bridge Street Shewing Tower · WD McLennan · Architect Paisley ·:

96) ST GEORGE'S UNITED FREE CHURCH – GORDON STREET. Inset photograph of W D McLENNAN ARCHITECT — This Church was built between 1905 and 1907, with funds raised by the congregation. William Daniel McLennan (1872-1940) rose to the challenge of designing one of Scotland's outstanding art nouveau buildings on a difficult corner site. Alas, the projected belfry tower was never built! McLennan was an elder in this Church and presented it with four communion cups. He became furious when the Church decided to remove his carefully designed wrought-iron work from the chancel (c1922) to permit a better view of a new memorial window. He left the Church soon afterwards. This Church is presently restored to its original glory.

97) PAISLEY RACES 1907 — The picture, with McFarlane Street in the back-ground, shows the last horse race held at Paisley Racecourse in 1907. The Course was condemned by the Jockey Club and The National Hunt Committee, as it did not have a straight stretch of five furlongs. Prior to this, the races took place between Love Street, St James Street and Caledonia Street, an area known as 'the twenty-four acres.' When the first race took place in 1620, the horses started at St Conval's Stone in Inchinnan, and ran through Renfrew, ending up at the Wallneuk of Paisley. Sadly the winning horse can no longer parade with the Paisley Silver Bells hung between its ears – Britain's oldest horse racing prize. Made in 1608 and first won by a Hew Crawford in 1620 they are now safely on show in Paisley Museum.

98) COATS OBSERVATORY, OAKSHAW 1910—Thomas Coats had always taken an interest in scientific pursuits and was a steady supporter of the local Philosophical Institution. In 1880 he provided funds for an astronomical telescope and an observatory to house it. His gift was transferred in 1892 to Paisley Philosophical Institution. The building, one of the earliest to have an internal ramped access, was formally opened in 1883 to designs by Honeyman. The buildings were further extended by James Coats, his son, in 1892. The building presently houses many valuable old instruments, including an equatorial telescope by Cook, Sidereal clock, an orrery, and various meteorological instruments. It is now run by Paisley Museum.

Paisley Clarion Cycling Club

99) PAISLEY CLARION CYCLING CLUB 1909 — Bicycles in Paisley proved popular with the middle-classes around the 1870s. The Paisley Amateur Club, founded in 1878, had forty members. This was followed, in 1879, by the founding of the Victoria Club with twenty members. In 1881, the Caledonia was formed with thirty members. Club meetings were generally held on Saturdays, between March and October. Club runs were generally limited to within twenty miles of Paisley. Touring excursions took place in August. Paisley around this time had seven bicycle shops and repairers. Alex Stevenson at the 'Sign of the Wheel', 29 Causeyside, was also a cycle-maker. The Paisley Clarion Cycling Club members were 'Clarion Scouts', a group of nascent Socialists who spread their political message using vans or cycles on various trips

Paisley.   Ferguslie Park.

100) FERGUSLIE PARK 1910 — This magnificent house was built for Sir Thomas Glen-Coats, in 1890, on the site of an old tower house. Thomas Glen-Coats was a staunch liberal and elected MP for Paisley in 1906. As the President of Paisley Liberal Club, he and his Canadian born wife entertained lavishly at their home. After the election hustings in 1926, when Asquith stood as Liberal candidate for Paisley, a party took place in this house. The main guests were Lord & Lady Asquith, Lloyd George and his daughter Megan, and Lady Bonham Carter. Asquith described the house as 'a typical millionaire's villa with some Corots, a Sir Joshua Reynolds, and a Hoppner intermixed with family photographs and some sentimental mezzotints'. In 1934 the house became an auxiliary hospital until finally closing down in 1972. It was demolished shortly after 1980.

101) COUNTY SQUARE 1911 — County Square wears the mantle of a military parade ground with Battalions of the local Argyll & Sutherland Highland Regiment lining the Square. To celebrate the coronation of King George V, they are firing a 'feu de joie' into the air. Gilmour Street, in the rear, is a mass of eager spectators – even an open top 'Glasgow caur' has been commandeered for the occasion. The Burgh Chambers to the right, have been dutifully decorated, with the Town Council appearing on the balcony. Note the solitary policeman in the picture!

102) JOHNSTON STREET FIRE STATION June 1911 — The men of Paisley Fire Brigade have decorated the station to celebrate the coronation of King George V. The gentleman in the centre was Arthur McNaughton, Paisley's first professional firemaster, appointed by the Town Council in 1877. The fire station, opened in April 1899, was designed to accommodate a newly acquired steam engine, two pipe carriages and a hand reel. It even had electric lighting and an alarm system built in. The total complement of men was seventeen, ten of whom stayed in the station. There were also stables to house at least four horses. This photograph also shows the last completely horse-drawn brigade, for a year later, in 1912, a motor fire engine which boasted a pump capacity of four-hundred-and-fifty gallons and a top speed of 40 mph was purchased.

103) GLENIFFER HOME YOUNG'S HORSE-DRAWN OMNIBUS c1912 — Young's horse-drawn omnibus service operated between the years 1894-1914. The route ran from County Square to Corsebar Road, Meikleriggs, its terminus, where the photograph was taken. Old Jimmy Wallace, the driver [noted for his punctuality], was well-known to his Paisley passengers! Notice the advert on the 'bus for the Thistle Carbolic Soap made locally by Isdale McCallum. The building to the left is Gleniffer Home. This house was bought and adapted as a home for people who were considered incurable, [by Archibald Coats of Woodside]. Opened in 1885 it originally accommodated eighteen patients and was maintained by public subscription. It is still used as an old folks' home today.

104) PAISLEY CROSS 1913 — A Glasgow open-top Car No.712, heading to Barrachnie, has just stopped at Paisley Cross. Barefoot boys stand astride the tramlines. Pupils with schoolbags and satchels hurry towards school. The Glasgow Savings Bank clock at Moss Street corner shows the time as 8.40 am. Birnie Rhinds statue (1889) of Sir Peter Coats stands sentinel over this busy scene. The building forming the corner to St Mirren Street was occupied by The National Bank of Scotland, whose blinds are still drawn. Above, the architect, Archibald Gibson had his office, while, further down St Mirren Street, the groundfloor shop of Cockburn the Chemist can be seen.

105) PAISLEY ABBEY: CLOISTERS — The two restored cloister walks were completed in 1915, to the design of Dr McGregor Chalmers. The design of the colonnade was determined by the discovery of some of the original 13th century capitals, taken from the East gable of the nave, when it was being removed in the restoration of 1898-1907. The photograph shows the foundation stone being laid by Mrs Archibald Craig, whose husband, a wealthy industrialist (third from right), had donated two-thousand pounds to restore the cloisters, in memory of-his father. Behind the ceremonial party, is the transition Norman doorway at the North-east corner of the cloister walk. It dates from around the first half of the 13th century.

106) CLARK'S MILL, SEEDHILL c1914 — Thousands of mill lassies have just finished their shift at the threadmills, adding an air of bustle and excitement to the street. Compared to their counterparts fifty years earlier, whose shoeless feet, jupe petticoats, and tartan shawls draped over their heads, these mill girls are neatly dressed in smart costumes, elegant hats, and have an air of prosperity. After all, the Paisley Mills were never 'dark satanic mills', but provided steady employment, liberal pay, and companionship to their thousands of employees.

107) CENTRAL HALLS, GAUZE STREET c1915 — The Wesleyan Methodist Central Halls were built in 1908. The size of the building reflects the strong hold that the Methodists had in Paisley from the end of the 18th century. Smithhills to the left (formerly New Smithhills) and its junction with Old Smithhills (now Gauze Street) was known in 1789 as Goudies cross. The name Smithhills dates back to the days when a smiddy was attached to the monastery. The earliest known smith to occupy this site before 1560 was John Luff.

108) POST OFFICE, COUNTY SQUARE 1915 — In 1751, Paisley's post office stood at the North corner of Moss Street and Meeting House Lane (The Dirty Steps).The Postmaster, Thomas Ker, had a small narrow booth as a post office which then formed part of a stationery shop. Larger premises were obtained at 5 Christie Terrace. In 1838, the post office was in Gilmour Street before moving to St Mirren Street in 1876. New buildings were opened in County Square adjoining Gilmour Street Station in 1893. Provost McGown, after opening the building, received a silver key presented by the main contractor, McNaughton. The building, designed in a Gothic Tudor style, boasted gas lighting and steam heating. The photograph shows the later baronial styled South wing, added in 1912.

109) SUCTION DREDGER LAUNCH – WHITE CART WATER 1917 — The shipbuilding business of John Fullerton & Company, Merksworth, was founded in 1867. The company was distinguished for building iron-steel cargo vessels, passenger steamers, pleasure yachts and tug steamers. The picture shows the launch of a suction dredger vessel at their yard in 1917. Spectators line the opposite bank of the narrow River Cart to see the launch performed by King George V. On the same day, he visited two other Paisley shipbuilding yards, where he launched a further two ships. Three launches on the same day was a record for the Cart! The business of John Fullerton & Co was to disappear in the 1920s, a casualty of the great depression.

110) 'THE PAISLEY HUT' 1919 — Photograph taken at Peronne (near Somme Battlefield, France) 1919. It shows one of the canteen huts organised by the YMCA for occupation forces shortly after the First World War. The group section probably comprised of Paisley men who had been workmates or chums and had volunteered for military service and formed, in many cases, sizeable units. On the extreme right is Corporal Robert Aiken, a dairyman from Broomlands and a Proud Paisley Patriot.

111) VISIT OF PRINCE OF WALES 10 March 1921 — In front of a large crowd of spectators in Abbey Close, Edward, Prince of Wales, prepares to enter the main entrance of the Town Hall for a Civic Reception. The gentleman to his left is Sir Thomas Glen-Coats, the Lord Lieutenant of Renfrewshire. Provost Lang in full regalia appears on the right.

112) ROYAL WELCOME – ANCHOR MILLS 1921 — A royal visit took place at the Seedhill Mill on 10 March 1921. The visitor was Edward, Prince of Wales (later Duke of Windsor). A crowd of millgirls and some of their children await the visit with excitement. The Gatehouse (erected 1909) has been dutifully draped in bunting, and two decorated archways have been erected over the Works entrance. At this time, this Mill employed around four-thousand girls, some of whom recalled that the Prince that day was a 'smasher'!

113) ABBEY WAR MEMORIAL 1923 — In the centre of the cloister garth stands the Abbey War Memorial unveiled by Earl Haig (extreme left) on 10 June 1923. The memorial is a replica of that designed by Sir Reginald Blomfield for the British War Cemeteries in France. Jeffrey Waddell was the supervising architect. Fifty-one men of the congregation had fallen in the Great War. Boy Scouts and Girl Guides line the cloisters.

114) DUNN STREET 1924 — This group photograph of East-end children was taken by an itinerant street photographer. The street consisted mainly of four storey, room and kitchen flats with half-landing toilets. Part of the street had 'wally closes'. The children are smartly turned out; some wear school caps, while older boys have neat collars and ties. The street games they played included hunch-cuddy-hunch (a form of leap frog against the tenement wall) and 'muggie' or marbles. Older boys would buy a penny-worth of sulphur potash, which was stuffed into a door key, rammed home with a nail, the impact against the tenement wall gave off a loud bang. During the depression, in 1926, some of these older children would go to the Bluebell Woods, to cut logs for the fire. Even the old avenue of trees in the back courts were removed for firewood, including the 'fat lady', the affectionate name for the oldest tree.

115) GLASGOW ROAD - LOOKING EAST 1920s — The bridge formed part of the Caledonian Paisley-Barrhead Railway, which began building around 1898. The high level station on the left-hand side of the bridge was known as Paisley East, and had been built on the site of a house called 'Glenham'. The railway was used as a goods line and for troop trains, during the First World War. The bridge was removed, together with Paisley East Station, in 1932, to make way for the Kelburne Cinema. The chemist shop (second from right), called the 'Sherwood Pharmacy', was owned by a Mr Inglis. One of his regular lady customers in buying lavender water, always insisted in asking for 'threepence-worth of lavatory water'!

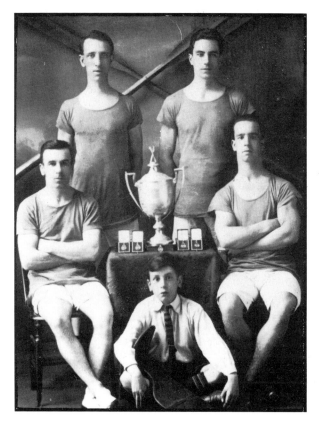

116) TRADES ROWING CLUB c 1924 — The Paisley Trades Rowing Club founded in 1885, formerly called 'The Calendermens' consisted of young artisans. They rowed on the lower stretch of the River Cart at the new harbour and held an annual regatta. The principal prizes competed for were, The Express Challenge Cup, awarded by William Lochhead of the Paisley Daily Express, and the Globe Challenge Cup, presented by A Morrison, late proprietor of the Globe Hotel. The only gentlemen identified in the picture are J.V.W. Brown (back row right), Robert Currie, Senior (seated left) and Robert Currie, Junior (front centre). They are sitting around the Express Challenge Trophy. This Club ceased to exist around 1926. Another club, the Linside, founded in 1810, rowed at the upper cart between Seedhill & Hawkhead, ceased around 1900.

Paisley War Memorial, Unveiled Sunday, 27th July, 1924

117) WAR MEMORIAL, PAISLEY CROSS 1924 — Paisley erected an equestrian statue as its War Memorial. Its designer Sir Robert Lorimer, together with Alice Meredith Williams (sculptress), won a design competition which had over two-hundred other entrants. The Memorial was unveiled on Sunday, 27 July 1924, by Mrs McNab, a local lady who had lost three sons in the war. Paisley lost nearly two thousand men in the Great War. One, Captain A Henderson VC MC, had the distinction of posthumously winning the Victoria Cross in 1917, at Fontaine-les-Croisilles, France. There is a model of this cenotaph in Cardiff City Museum.

Barshaw Tennis Courts, Paisley

118) BARSHAW PARK TENNIS COURT c1925 — In 1912 the town acquired the former estate of James Arthur of Barshaw and turned it into a public park. In addition to a bandstand and boating pond, the tennis courts proved popular. The lady tennis players are wearing long skirts and cloche hats. The wooden pavilion behind, served as a ticket office and a tearoom. In 1941, a Luftwaffe bomb exploded in the park, just behind the row of trees but fortunately no-one was killed. In 1881, the Stanley Lawn Tennis Club was formed, playing at Greenlaw Drive. That year, on 17 July, Sergeant Heiton, a local man, won the coveted St George's Vase at Wimbledon. Before 1653, Paisley's earliest 'real tennis' court or 'caitchpool' was in existence. It was situated in a converted cornhouse near the North-west corner of Abbey Close.

119) ST MIRREN FC SCOTTISH CUP WINNERS SEASON 1925-1926 — At the 1926 Scottish Cup Final, a crowd of 100,000 saw Davie McCrae (front row centre) score St Mirren's first goal, within three minutes, at Hampden Park, against the redoubtable Glasgow Celtic. After twenty-five minutes, Howieson (front row second from right) scored St Mirren's second goal. It was all over! Celtic had no reply! St Mirren had avenged their first ever Cup Final appearance in 1907-08 season, when they were beaten by Celtic. Up to this point in the Club's history, apart from winning the local Renfrewshire Cup, they had won the Victory Cup in 1919 in an extra-time affair by whipping Hearts 3-0. In 1921 the Barcelona Cup, a magnificent trophy, won on a match tour in Spain, found its way back to Paisley.

120) PAISLEY CURLERS, LOCHWINNOCH c1925 — Paisley curlers have played at Castle Semple Loch since at least 1784. The town's earliest club, called 'The Sandholes' was started in 1795. The Sneddon Club began in 1815. Contemporary with them was the Storie Street Club. By 1829, these Clubs joined up to form the Paisley United Curling Club. Between 1841 and 1856, the Paisley Iceland, Paisley Union, St Mirren, Boreas, and Renfrewshire Clubs were formed. In earlier days when hard frost appeared it was the custom for Paisley's Town Drummer to proclaim to the citizens of Paisley, in the evening, the venues for the next day's curling matches. Paisley can boast of the earliest known recorded game of curling. This took place on 6 February 1541, between John Sclater, a monk at Paisley Abbey, and Gavin Hamilton. It was a challenge match, which took place on the ice lying West of the Abbot's room at a place called Horgart.

121) H H ASQUITH - PAISLEY MP 1920-1926 — In 1920, Asquith stood for Paisley, always a Liberal stronghold. He won the seat by a majority of nearly three-thousand votes. Although he won two more elections at Paisley, the last, in 1926, was held by a majority of only three-hundred-and-sixteen votes. Biggar, his Labour opponent, lost by a narrow squeak. The hustings of 1926 were described by Asquith thus 'I have rarely felt less exhilaration than when we got to the platform, amid wild plaudits'. This last election is now only remembered in a Paisley child's skipping rhyme:

Vote for Asquith, The man you know.
In to parliament, He should go.
If Mr Biggar says a word,
We'll hit him on the head with a horse's club.

122) JAMES ROBERTSON & SONS: GOLDEN SHRED — In 1864 a young grocer, James Robertson, and his wife, Marion, found they had a barrel of bitter oranges left on their hands. Marion turned the surplus stock into marmalade using her own unique recipe. This marmalade called 'Golden Shred' was an immediate success. Their first shop was set up in Causeyside Street. Later, the company moved to Thrushgrove Works in Stevenson Street. By 1890, the output had reached several hundred tons annually at Paisley, so another factory was opened in 1891 at Manchester, and by the end of the century at Catford in London. In 1910, John Robertson, the founder's son, who had been on a trip to America, was intrigued there by the current craze for golliwogs. He brought one home, and, for some reason or another, the golliwog became the firm's trademark. In 1914, a factory was opened in Bristol. At this time the firm was the world's largest preserve manufacturers. Sadly the Paisley factory was closed, and Scottish Power offices have occupied the site since 1979.

123) THE RUSSELL INSTITUTE 1927 — Paisley's new clinic was opened in March 1927 by HRH Princess Mary. Miss Agnes Russell had gifted money to build a clinic in memory of her two brothers. The site purchased formed part of the old lands of Aiket's Yard and had contained some old tenements and shops. One person who had a business interest there was 'Doo Broon', a noted troublesome character, who initially refused to move out but after some delay, work began on the new building in 1924. The architect was J Steel Maitland (standing left side of picture) wearing a wide brimmed hat. Maitland (1887-1982), was apprenticed to William Leiper. In 1908, he emigrated to Canada. He became a pilot during the First World War and in 1919 returned to Scotland to establish his own firm – Rocus Toys of Paisley, whose clients included Heals and Liberty's of London. In 1923, he became a partner with T G Abercrombie and sole partner in 1925.

Paisley Abbey as it will appear when the Restoration is completed.

124) PAISLEY ABBEY 1928 — It took from 1788-1928 for the Abbey Church to be finally restored. From an early attempt in 1788, the first major restoration began between 1859 and 1862, when the nave and North transept were restored. Dr Rowand Anderson, architect from 1898-1907, reinforced the tower foundation and piers and erected the tower just beyond the nave roof. Under Chalmers (1912-1922) and later Lorimer (1922-1928), the choir walls and roof were built, together with the tower. A spire was never built, as it was considered unsafe. By 1933, the surroundings were cleaned up and landscaped. This Church is the jewel in Paisley's crown and it is a tribute to its townspeople, that such a vast undertaking was successfully completed.

125) PAGEANT OF PAISLEY 1929 — The picture shows the 'finale' of the Pageant of Paisley held in the Town Hall in 1929. This was the climax of a musical pageant which, in twelve scenes, re-enacted episodes of Paisley's history. The costumes were designed by J Steel Maitland, a local architect, and the script written by Dr Stewart Black, a noted local historian and Scottish playwright. The two hundred or so cast comprised mainly young people. One young man, David K Hamilton appeared as a minstrel. He was later to use his acting ability to escape, dressed as a French Officer, from the infamous Colditz Castle prisoner-of-war camp, during WWII.

126) NEW ALEX CINEMA 1929 — The New Alex cinema, built in the 1920s, stood at the corner of Orr Street and Neilston Road. The picture shows excited children in a queue and about to see their 'Saturday heroes' in the cinema. The boys wear school caps and heavy leather boots with thick wool socks. One wee boy has no shoes at all! The commissionaire is busy keeping the children in line. They are totally unaware that they were being filmed at this time. The film would be shown at this cinema a few days later to encourage others to flock to the cinema. The photograph is a 'still' from this film, which was called "The Children's Happy Hunting Ground". It was presented to the Scottish Film Archive for preservation by the Old Paisley Society and it is held by this Archive for the Society.

127) GLEN CINEMA PRIOR TO DEMOLITION c1930 — The cinema [opened in 1910], known as 'The Glen' and 'The Royal Animated Pictures', once formed part of the Good Templar Halls as was occupied by Burton's shop. On the afternoon of 31 December 1929, during a children's matinee, a freshly shown film put in its metal box in the spool room began to issue thick black smoke. Soon the smoke filled the auditorium containing about one thousand children. Panic set in. Children ran downstairs so fast and in such numbers, that they piled up behind the escape door which led to Dyers Wynd. The door could not be opened, as it was designed to open inwards. The following day, Paisley was stunned by the news that seventy children had died in the crush in the worst cinema disaster in British history. The irony was, there was no actual fire.

Clarks, they have the anchor.
Coats, they have the chain.
Paisley has the cotton trade
and long may it remain.

128) FERGUSLIE MILLS 1930 — This aerial view looking North shows the sixty acre complex occupied by Ferguslie Thread Mills. From a small factory erected there by James Coats in 1826 the premises grew to gigantic proportions. By the end of the century, combining with their old rivals the Clarks, the business became the world's largest threadworks. The buildings, mainly designed by Woodhouse & Newley in the 1880s, were hailed as Scotland's finest threadmills. The last surviving large building, the old No. 1 Spinning Mill (right of picture) was demolished in 1992. Coats trademark, a chain, and Clark's, the anchor, are remembered in the skipping song above.

129) CHARLESTON 1930 — Neilston Road runs left to right at the top of this aerial view. The original South School built in 1877 hides behind its later addition and sits at the corner of New Stock Street. Old Stock Street, its continuation, is flanked by Charleston Bowling Club (founded 1864) and by the pavilions of the Royal Alexandra Infirmary (erected 1900) built on the lands of Egypt Park. The village of Charleston began with the erection of small two storey terraced houses called Thom's Buildings, fronting Old Stock Street and Neilston Road junction. Charles Thom, a builder, developed this area by 'rearing houses like mushrooms' in or about 1815. Charleston was called after him. More houses were built in Great Hamilton Street, with Union Street connecting it to Old Stock Street.

130) NEILSTON ROAD 1930 — The Charleston Clock Tower, in the distance, was erected in 1887. The buildings underneath, erected in 1886, were the first tenements in Paisley to have internal WCs. The WCs formed part of the original design. The Town Council debated long and hard and considered that inside toilets would become a nuisance to the occupants, however, they reluctantly approved the design. Carriagehill, further up, was the old name for this part of Neilston Road. The lands of Carriagehill were first mentioned in 1218 when they formed part of the tocher of King Alexander Ill's daughter. The range of buildings to the right, running downhill to Rowan Street, formed the steadings of Kilncroft, first developed and built by Charles Thom and Robert Rowan about 1776.

131) TWO MILL GIRLS, HIGH STREET 1930 — A typical 'walkie' photograph taken outside The Picture House Cinema. Built between 1911 and 1913, was described in the 30s as "Paisley's wonder cinema" having Western Electric Sound. It showed not only early sound films, but contained a magnificent Art Deco foyer complete with fountain, and a large cafe restaurant. The two girls, Margaret Robertson from Kilnside Road (left) and Jeanette Crawford from 'Wee Seedhill Road' had started work in the Anchor Mills when they were fourteen. Margaret was a 'runner' in the ticketing department. Jeanette also worked there. Both girls wear black 'military look' jackets, knee-length tweed skirts, and suede court shoes. Margaret also wears a beret and black leather gloves.

132) CAMPHILL SENIOR SECONDARY SCHOOL 1930   INSET PHOTO JOHN TAYLOR — Camphill Public School (originally to be called Victoria School) was opened on 14 April 1888. It was the largest school in Scotland, designed for an intake of two thousand pupils. Up to this time around one-thousand-and-four-hundred local children were uneducated through lack of school places. Camphill met this need and by 1894 had a roll of 2,500 pupils. To ensure the early success of the school, John Taylor was appointed as headmaster. Since 1871, he had been made headmaster of each new board school opened. Under Taylor's rule, Camphill was elevated to a higher grade school in 1904. By 1925, the first Secondary IV class had appeared. After 1928, the primary department disappeared. It was thereafter known as Camphill Senior Secondary and remained so until 1967. It was demolished in 1969.

133) KELBURNE CINEMA 1933 — This cinema, opened on 27 November 1933, had a facade of marmino, a special kind of brightly coloured terrazzo, and at night it was illuminated by an extensive neon sign. It had a seating capacity of 1784 including stalls and balcony and contained a first class lounge and cafe. The deep stage was designed for variety entertainment, with artistes dressing rooms on each side. Admission was seven pence for front stalls, one shilling for stalls, and one shilling and sixpence for back circle. The first film shown was 'Heads We Go' and featured Constance Cummings. In order to build the cinema, part of the old Barracks were vacated and the old railway bridge across Glasgow Road was removed, together with Paisley East Station.

134) THOMAS SMITH TAIT 1882-1952 — Educated at Paisley's John Neilson Institution and apprenticed to a local architect James Donald, Tait studied at the Glasgow School of Art. In 1901 he gained a prize for ornamental design – the only one that came to Scotland that year. In 1902 he won the King's Prize for architecture. As a member of Paisley YMCA Canal Street Branch, he is described that year as 'designing large articles', probably destined to appear in a Grand Bazaar to be held in Paisley Town Hall in aid of the proposed new YMCA HQ buildings in Paisley. Tait became the most prominent Scots architect between the wars and was in the forefront of British modernism. He designed Adelaide House 1921-24, Daily Telegraph Office 1927, St. Andrews's House, Edinburgh 1934, and in 1932 won the competition for Hawkhead ID Hospital, Paisley. He was best known as the controlling designer at Glasgow's Empire Exhibition, 1938, where Tait's Tower dominated the scene.

135) HAWKHEAD HOSPITAL 1937 — Thomas Tait won, by competition in 1932, the commission to design Hawkhead Infectious Diseases Hospital. He was the most prominent Scots architect of the inter-war years and had achieved a global reputation. In July 1936, this hospital was opened to replace the old, outdated fever hospital at Bridge Street. The streamlined white pavilions and their layout was hailed by medical delegations from all over Britain as a triumph of architecture combined with efficiency and utility. During its first twenty years, it played an important role in the eradication of tuberculosis, but with the introduction of more modern medicines not long after it opened, its concept of having separate pavilions became unnecessary.

136) PAISLEY 1938 — The White Cart Water stank with pollution and was infested with rats. Despite the health hazards, the old Bladda fever hospital had once occupied the vacant site on the left bank. Cart Walk, on the right bank, followed the river to its junction with the bridge and a tavern called 'The Lighthouse'. The large works of Charles Glasgow, an eminent coachbuilder, lies behind Cart Walk. Thread Street appears on the extreme right of the picture. In the distance, the rebuilt Abbey Close Church appears in front of the Town Hall. This little building, apart from having association with the famous David Dale, was also associated with Charles Rennie Mackintosh, as he designed its organ casing and pulpit

137) BACK COURT, 20 Andrews Street 1935 — Having a photograph taken was a special event for these children. The occasion is marked with a card saying 'Chums 1935'. This tenement housed eleven families in one close. The flats were room and kitchen type with bed recesses. Toilets were confined to the half-landings. A girl on the left stands astride her scooter – a favourite toy in these days. The older bereted girl, wearing a shawl collar coat, is Jean McGuire. In front of her is Alastair Irwin wearing a baby harness. The boys all wear short trousers. One in the front row, clutches his cherished, 'tube and cover' football.

138) ARCHIE McKELLAR DSO DFC and BAR 1912-1940 — Paisley's 'forgotten air ace' of WWII was born in 1912 at 4 Southpark Drive. A plaque outside this tenement close was placed there in 1992. It describes him simply as a 'Battle of Britain Pilot'. He gained his RAF wings and joined the City of Glasgow 602 Fighter Squadron in 1936 as a Flying Officer. In less than a year he was made a Squadron Leader. In October 1939, in action over the Firth of Forth, he shot down one of the first Heinkel aircraft of the war. His cool head and reckless courage made him the scourge of the Luftwaffe. When he destroyed 8 German 'planes over a period of 8 days, he was awarded a Bar to his DFC. He was now famous throughout fighter Command. On 31st October 1940 – the official end of the Battle of Britain – Air Marshal Dowding mentioned McKellar in despatches. McKellar was killed in action the following day over Kent and so was not listed in the roll of honour of the Battle. He is now, if belatedly, recognised as being the most successful pilot of the Battle of Britain.

139) FIRST AID POST NO.5 – GEORGE STREET 1940 — This was the original First Aid Post No. 5 hurriedly built in George Street, adjoining the rear of the old West School whose sand-bagged windows are seen in the picture. At the door stands a bowler hatted adjutant and a nurse. John Marshall (left) initially based at this Post was transferred to Woodside Post No. 5, which replaced the one in the picture. In May 1941 John lost a leg when a Luftwaffe landmine landed on that Station. He luckily survived, unlike the other 92 unfortunate victims. That same night, a second bomb landed in Newton Street killing another two persons.

140) PAISLEY ABBEY CHORISTERS 1943 — A sang schule existed as part of the early 'Grammar Schule' and provided something in the way of choral services in the Abbey. In 1807, R A Smith, a gifted and noted musician and composer, was appointed precentor in the Abbey. He re-shaped the Abbey band, first founded in 1795 by Dr Boag, and soon, with its soft singing, the unique 'band' became famous throughout Scotland. The boy choristers were first robed in scarlet cassocks and white surplices in 1921, at the dedication of the new choir stalls. On its completion in 1928, men and women of the choir were likewise robed. The choirmaster in 1943 was Alfred Wilson. Paisley Abbey choir is today one of Scotland's leading choirs and is under the able leadership of George McPhee, organist and Master of Choristers.

141) BACK COURT, SCHOOL WYND 1946 — In older areas of the town, back courts were often narrow and ill-lit. Despite these conditions, this Paisley housewife, dressed in a period cross-over pinny, attempts to hang out her washing between coal cellars and the brick wash-house on the right. The dark low door, lit by an overhead gas light, led to the older styled stone turret stair of this tenement.

142) MOSS STREET c1946 — Cocooned Grumman Avenger fighter aircraft have just emerged from St. James Street (right) and are turning into Old Sneddon Street. They had been towed from the nearby Fleet Air Arm station based at Abbotsinch, where HMS SANDERLING gave sterling service during World War II. This base closed in 1962 to make way for Glasgow Airport. Steam can be seen from a train crossing the Moss Street railway bridge. The buildings on the left, forming St. James Place, have long since been removed.

143) BRIDGE STREET 1946 — On the site of the old Bridge Street Fever Hospital, these bomb shelters had been erected during the Second World Ward. The area was used also as a 'bus depot. Behind is Cart Walk running parallel to the River Cart and terminating at the large white building the premises of Thomas Reid & Sons, engineers,windlass, steering gear, and capstan makers. Sherwood Church spire looms in the distance. The area behind Cart Walk was cleared to house the local government buildings erected in 1969.

144) TA TA BELLA (JAMES PURDIE) — Ta Ta Bella, alias Saturday Johnnie, was a well-known worthy in the district, between the 1930s-50s. His sad grey bearded face was capped by an old soft hat, which flopped over his ears. Underneath his two well-worn overcoats was an old jacket. His last visible garment was a collarless shirt. Over his shoulder, he always carried a sack used as a receptacle for 'jeely' jars and lemonade bottles (then redeemable for pennies.) His days were spent in tenement back courts raking the middens, after which he would announce himself to the occupants, by first performing a little dance and then launching into song – 'Ta Ta Bella, I'll no say goodbye Although I'm leaving Glasgow with the HLI' Having collected his rewards of money, jam jars, and lemonade bottles, he would leave followed by a crowd of children chanting : - "Ta Ta Bella, yer bum's a' yella" –

145) VIEW FROM JAIL TOWER January 1947 — Left of the River Cart stands Paisley Theatre. Water Brae runs alongside. Ta Ta Bella squatted here. The old house (formerly 2 New Smithhills) between the theatre and St James Bridge was once owned by Miss Kibble of Greenlaw, who founded the Ragged School and the Kibble Reformatory (opened 1859). Alexander Gardner, printer, had his business in the building (bottom right) in Dyers Wynd. The Town Hall and Abbey appear in the distance. The site now forms part of Paisley Piazza.

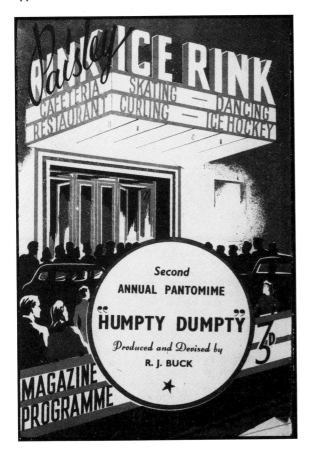

146) PAISLEY ICE RINK PROGRAMME 1947 — This shows the main entrance to Paisley Ice Rink. Built on the site of Ralston Park Football ground and opened in 1940 at East Lane, it was advertised as the most up-to-date winter sports stadium in Britain. Soon it played to packed houses with ice-hockey matches, ice pantomimes, skating, tennis matches, figure skating championships, wrestling and boxing (Cassius Clay appeared here). By the late 1960s, it began to make losses. In April 1970 it closed, ostensibly for repairs. In November that year, only professional wrestling took place. Shortly after 1973, the building was closed and replaced by a supermarket.

147) GIBSON'S TEAROOM, 16 HIGH STREET c1947 — Andrew Gibson & Son were well-known bakers, restaurateurs and purveyors in Paisley. Their business had been founded in 1838. In 1899 the firm employed a local architect to design their new shop-front at their High Street premises. He was W D McLennan, whose offices were in the nearby Masonic Buildings at 96 High Street. His new design, to say the least, was radical and must have turned a few heads. The frontage consisted of a tea-room designed in the Glasgow style and a shop with magnificent art nouveau attenuated joinery. It is a pity that McLennan's design was removed to make way for a modern Woolworth building.

148) 'SATURDAY NIGHT HOP' PAISLEY TOWN HALL 1948 — The Town Hall became a public dance hall on a Saturday night. The young men were dressed in their best suits with collar and tie, hair plastered in 'Brilliantine'. The girls usually wore sweaters, a waspie belt around their waists, and long pleated skirts. Although the town had no purpose built ballrooms, young people had the choice of 'The Big Co', 'The Wee Co', or 'The Templars'. Between 1910 and 1930, most young men and women attended Billy Primrose's classes in Forbes Place, and would dance at the Paisley Plaza (later to become St Charles Chapel) in Neilston Road. The Plaza was the mecca of more accomplished dancers, and had the attraction that dance hostesses were provided.

149) McCRACKEN'S DANCE BAND 1948 — Paisley's most popular dance band was formed in 1946, just after the war, by Jim McCracken. He was the pianist in the picture. The singer was Margaret Wallace. The band, a twelve piece orchestra, photographed in the Town Hall in 1948, was Paisley's 'big band'. Due to costs, the band became smaller, having three or four players in 1958. When Jim McCracken died in 1968, his widow, Ella, a musician in her own right, took over the band. They were familiar faces at the Brabloch Hotel for many years.

150) DANISH STONE 1950 — This old stone once stood at the North-west Corner of 'Stanely Green Shaw'. In 1902 it was moved, to make way for the Paisley-Barrhead railway, to its present site just South of Stanely Castle, seen in the background. In 1782, Semple, a local historian called it the 'Danish Stone' thinking it dated back to Viking times and perhaps marked the site of a battle. It was however undoubtedly an early Christian Cross. All that remains today, is its base and Part of the shaft. As Paisley Abbey, in medieval times, was on one of the pilgrim routes, this cross no doubt guided travellers to and from Ayrshire towards the Shrine of St Mirin.

151) BLACKHALL MANOR HOUSE c1950 — Walter, founder of Paisley Abbey and First High Steward of Scotland, built a house upstream from the waterfall of the River Cart, on the lands of Blackhall, next to the forest of Hunterhill. In 1165, it was described as being 'above the rock where my hall was built'. It became the local Royal hunting lodge, and had its chapel nearby. Two humble men connected with the household were Thomas the Brewer, who was allowed to graze his cattle in the Park of Blackhall (1294) and Thomas, a wright of Blakehall (1296). King Robert III granted the house and land to his natural son, John Stewart, in 1396. Through time, the house devolved to the Shaw-Stewarts of Ardgowan. Around 1560, the house was rebuilt to its present form. In 1978, the building was scheduled for demolition, but protests by interested groups helped save it. By 1982-83, it had been completely restored into a private house.

152) HAWKHEAD HOUSE, PAISLEY c1950 — The Ross family first obtained Hawkhead in 1367. Around the medieval tower house Lord James Ross, in 1634, added further buildings and laid out large orchards with fine terraced gardens, the first Dutch garden in Renfrewshire. In 1681, the Duke of York (later King James II) dined at the 'Halcat' (Hawkhead House) with Lord Ross. Through marriage, Hawkhead devolved on the Earl of Glasgow. In 1782, the Countess of Glasgow made great repairs and improvements to the house, adding a new 120-ft long greenhouse. Behind this stood an ice house, the only one in the County, In 1886, the house was owned by a William Stevenson, and in 1914 it became a mental hospital, By 1948, the house neglected, fell into disrepair and was finally demolished in 1953.

153) TANNAHILL'S COTTAGE, QUEEN STREET, PAISLEY, c1950 — In 1775 James Tannahill, a bien weaver, acquired a steading in Queen Street and built on it a one storey thatched cottage which served on one side as a living quarter, and as a four loom weaving shop on the other. The cost of building, including drink money for the workmen, was £60. Apart from a brief spell working in Bolton, it was here that his son Robert the poet lived his life and wrote his poems. The building was gifted to Paisley Burns Club in 1933 and opened formally in 1936. It is the meeting place of Paisley Burns Club (instituted 1805), the Tannahill-MacDonald Club (instituted 1874) and the Bohemian Club (instituted 1895),

154) LOU COSTELLO AT 117 SEEDHILL ROAD 1951 — Abbott & Costello had been appearing at the Glasgow Empire Theatre. Lou Costello, with his wife Ann Baxter, a Paisley lass and her three daughters, took the opportunity to visit Ann's Paisley relatives. Lou and Christine, one of his daughters, sit on the steps of 117 Seedhill Road, the home of the McKechnie family, and cousins of Ann. They are standing behind the Hollywood star in the house doorway. After this, he visited 2 Unsted Place, to meet more relations, Mr & Mrs George Connell and their son David who was ill in bed. To complete his visit, Lou treated the Paisley relatives to a slap-up meal in Glasgow's 101 Restaurant.

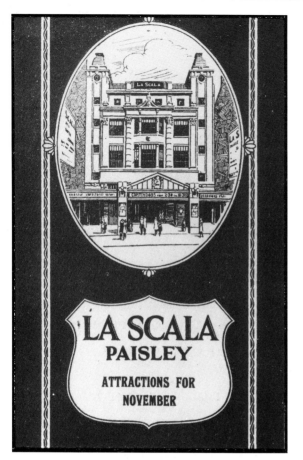

155) LA SCALA CINEMA c1950 — Paisley's 'Refined Cinema' opened in 1921. In 1929, it advertised its 'supreme talkie reproduction'. By 1930, it advertised a 'miniature golf course' for use of its patrons – the only one in Scotland! When the La Scala first opened, competition was fierce. Nearby was the Paisley Picture Theatre in the High Street. Opposite this was the Picture Palace. The Town Hall showed the 'C C' pictures. The Rink (Astoria) was in Lawn Street. The Royal Animated Pictures used part of the Good Templar Halls. In addition, there were 'Castle Pictures' and the Palladium. Even the Paisley Theatre showed films. The 'Rat Pit', better known as the Empire Music Hall, in Moss Street had the distinction of first showing 'lumiere' type films in 1895. The La Scala of the 50s saw Saturday night queues stretching down St. Mirin's Brae despite the other 7 cinemas in the town. Littlewood's store now stands on the site of the much missed La Scala.

156) HIGH STREET/PAISLEY CROSS, August 1953 — A Renfrew Ferry bound tramcar turns into Gilmour Street. Adjoining the Bank building, the distinguished old shopfront of the Maypole Dairy is seen. Behind the tramcar is the 20s styled marbled entrance to the La Scala Cinema. Above this, a large gable advert reads 'La Scala – First with the latest – Hear clearly here'. The building between the cinema and Marks & Spencer contained, until last year when they were demolished, the City Bakeries shop and tearoom. The La Scala was removed several years ago to make way for a Littlewood store, and the Maypole Dairy has long since disappeared.

157) QUEEN'S CORONATION TOUR June 1953 — Crowds began to assemble at five o'clock in the morning in County Square. They carried stools, flasks of tea and lemonade to sustain them until the arrival of the royal party. The Queen and Prince Philip arrived by train at a newly painted Gilmour Street Station and emerged into a large cheering crowd in County Place, lined with policemen and personnel from HMS 'SANDERLING'. The Queen was greeted at the old Municipal Buildings by civic dignitaries. There she signed the visitors book before driving past the Cross and along Glasgow Road. The route was lined with schoolchildren who had been given a holiday. The tour ended at Balfron Road, Oldhall, where she saw houses newly built by The Scottish War Veterans Garden City Association.

158) PAISLEY PIRATES ICE HOCKEY TEAM SEASON 1953-54 — Paisley Ice Rink opened in 1940. Ice Hockey soon had the large arena swarming with thousands of fans. The Paisley Pirates, whose early teams were mainly Canadian, were the epitome of the game in Scotland. In the year this photograph was taken, they had won the Autumn Cup, the Scottish League, and the Canada Cup. Their success brought them to the British League, but local supporters could ill afford to travel down South and gradually support waned. The Junior team, the Wildcats, were wound up, followed by the Pirates. The Mohawks replaced them, but could not regenerate the enthusiasm of the Pirates. In 1970 the ice rink closed to ice sports.

159) BACK COURT, 9 BARR STREET April 1954 — This building was demolished, shortly after the picture was taken, to make way for the George Street/Canal Street comprehensive redevelopment plan. In 1954 this old area of the town consisted of 880 such houses with a population of 2900. Overcrowded, of low sanitary category, the houses were of one or two room dwellings. This two storey rubble built house, with turret stair, was built around 1820 and housed four families. The brick toilets are a later addition. Notice the 50s style prams, and the girl wearing a typical period Peter-Pan coat.

160) 'UP THE BRAES', GLENFIELD ROAD c1956 — A walk up the Gleniffer Braes had been popular among the weaving community of Paisley, since the time of Robert Tannahill. His poem 'The Braes of Gleniffer' immortalised this area. Following in his footsteps, Hugh MacDonald (1817-1860), the Glasgow poet, made this walk popular by his book, 'Rambles round Glasgow', published in 1854. His poem, 'The Bonnie Wee Well on the Breist o' the Brae', is inscribed at the present MacDonald Well, erected in 1883, further up the Brae. In the 1940s-50s, this walk was particularly popular after Sunday Church Service. In the distance below, Glenburn housing scheme was built, following a Burgh development plan approved in June 1953.

161) PAISLEY CROSS 1957 — An Elderslie No.146 hex-dash standard tram has just left the special loading island, built in the middle of the street. These were used for tram queues during rush hours. A Western 'red' 'bus, parked on the left side of the street, awaits passengers heading for Glasgow. Its registration, XS 6906, indicates that it had formerly belonged to Young's 'buses and would have had an original orange livery. A plethora of overhead electric contact wires serve the tramcars at this busy junction. The railings around the two statues of Peter and Thomas Coats have long since been removed. Behind the statues can be seen the magnificent Clark Town Hall.

162) LAST TRAM - PAISLEY CROSS 22 May 1957 — Some four thousand Buddies gathered at Paisley Cross to say goodbye to Paisley's last tram. While crowds awaited its arrival from Renfrew, an enterprising citizen in full Highland costume entertained them to a Highland Fling, dancing across the tram lines! Souvenir hunters aboard the tram stripped it of anything that could be pocketed. As the tram arrived, around one o'clock in the morning, it had an escort of a hundred private cars driving behind with lights blazing and horns tooting. Paisley Cross had not witnessed such crowds, since VE night.

163) ST MIRREN FC SEASON 1958-59 — After defeating Celtic 4-0 in the semi-final of the Scottish Cup at Hampden St Mirren met Aberdeen in the final. A crowd of 108,000, of which 60,000 were 'Buddies' including wee boys, grannies and mill girls (who kept fainting)! St Mirren won the day 3-1. St Mirren created football history the following season, by beating Glasgow University 15-0 in a Scottish Cup tie. The history was made by St Mirren's Gerry Baker scoring ten of the goals - no one, this century in Scotland, had ever scored so many in a major competition!

164) MOSS STREET c1958 — This narrow, old medieval street originally led to Paisley Moss and the Sneddon area. The street had various names in the past – Moss Raw, Moss Gait, Wangate End. In the early days, when Paisley was a little burgh, the street was protected by a port called Moss Raw Port. The picture shows two fashionably dressed ladies walking towards the Cross. Above them are the old Exchange Rooms which were built in 1837 on the site of the old flesh-market. Notice the hand-barrow used by tradesmen and builders to transport materials to a job.

165) PAISLEY MUSICAL & OPERATIC SOCIETY 1959 — This, the oldest surviving music society in Paisley, was founded in 1908 by a small Masonic company who first met in the George Temperance Hotel. Their first production, 'The Mikado', took place in Paisley Theatre in 1908. During the 30s their productions were mainly Gilbert & Sullivan operas, which took place in the Town Hall and the Templars Hall. After the war they returned to Paisley Theatre, where their last show, 'Princess Ida', in 1959 was held. The finale is illustrated in this photograph. The Society still regularly appears at the King's Theatre, Glasgow.

166) VICTORY THEATRE, PAISLEY 1960 — Mr Brickwell's new theatre (built in 1890 in New Smithhills Street) had the distinction of being the first fireproof theatre built outside London. The London architects, Crewe & Sprague, had overlooked the fact that the dressing rooms, built next to the River Cart, flooded when it was in spate! The opening performance was given by the Paul Jones Opera Company. Appearances by George Robey were popular, but the young Harry Lauder was often booed off stage! Between 1921 and 1934 the theatre showed mainly variety and repertory. After the Second World War, appearances of the Logan family ensured full houses. In 1959 the theatre closed, with the final curtain coming down on the Boy Scouts of Paisley Gang Show. The theatre was demolished in 1967.

167) FLOOD – STOCKHOLM CRESCENT c1963 — Completed between 1946 and 1947, this was the first, new, post-war Council housing scheme in Paisley. It consisted wholly of Swedish timber houses, set in an appropriately named Stockholm Crescent. To the delight of local children, the street was badly flooded most winters, due to its proximity to the Espedair Burn. Certainly Stephen Young, seen crossing the street, appears to be nearly above his welly tops! The Burn was later culverted by the Corporation.

168) WILLIAM GALLACHER (1881-1965) — Born in Paisley's 'Wee Sneddon' on Christmas Day 1881, Willie, fifty-four years later became the second Communist MP in Britain. Leaving Camphill School at the age of twelve, he first became a grocer's delivery boy and then a ship's steward with the misfortune of being shipwrecked on his first voyage. Via the Temperance Movement and The Social Democratic Federation, he entered politics. Soon at the forefront, he was to meet Lenin in 1920 after which he helped found the British Communist Party eventually becoming its president between 1956 and 63. During the First World War he was an active 'Red Clydesider'. He founded the Shops Steward Movement, found time to write poetry and publish several books including 'Revolt on the Clyde' and 'The Case for Communism'. He was known locally as a ' decent wee man' respected and loved by citizens of Paisley. His mile long funeral cortege – Paisley's largest this century – testified to this.

169) THE PAISLEY POLYTECHNIC, 36-38 HIGH STREET c1956 — This austere building typified the mid-Victorian textile warehouses built in various parts of the town, mainly to serve the shawl industry. Naismith & Scott, an old family firm, ran a wholesale and retail drapery here. The shop specialised in millinery and children's clothes. The 'Shoe Corner' at the top of New Street replaced a bookshop/lending library known as the 'Pen Corner', denoted by a large fountain pen shop-sign.

170) FERGUSLIE MILLS SKAILING c1957 — Mill girls spill through the factory gates into Maxwellton Street. Underneath their headscarves, the younger girls often wore curlers to be ready 'for the dancin' that evening. When a mill girl was to be married, her workmates paraded her through the town dressed in paper rosettes and streamers. She was made to carry a chamber-pot full of salt for good luck. Lifelong friendships were often formed with ex-mill girls still meeting regularly for 'knitting or sewing bees' years after the mills were closed.

171) WILLIAM McCULLOCH c1958 — Paisley had its own 'Oor Willie' McCulloch. From an early age, elocution and theatricals were in his blood. After serving as the local Collector of Rates until 1927, he turned professional entertainer and broadcaster often topping the bill at concerts in London, Edinburgh and Glasgow, where his audiences grew to love this 'master of voices' who told funny tales in the true West of Scotland genre. His recordings, now collectors items, were many and include such gems as 'When Agnes got Married', 'The Singing Lesson', or 'Follow Follow' recorded in 1928 after a Rangers win over Celtic in the Scottish Cup. McCulloch himself, of course, was St Mirren daft!

172) FLEMING & FERGUSON, SHIPBUILDERS 1878-1968 — Fleming & Ferguson, founded in 1878, had entered the world of shipbuilding in the White Cart Water as a latecomer but quickly established their reputation for specialising in dredgers, steam yachts, marine and land engines. At the turn of the century, making formidable ice-breakers became part of the yard's repertoire. During WWI the yard boomed. By the outbreak of WWII the yard saw its 'finest hours' building six powerful tugs, nine corvettes, five frigates, four armed trawlers, one minesweeper, two rescue craft and four crane steamers which were used in the Normandy D-day landings. Their best known ship was the 'John Biscoe', a research ice-breaker used in the 1956 Antarctic Expedition. This, Paisley's last shipyard, closed in 1968.

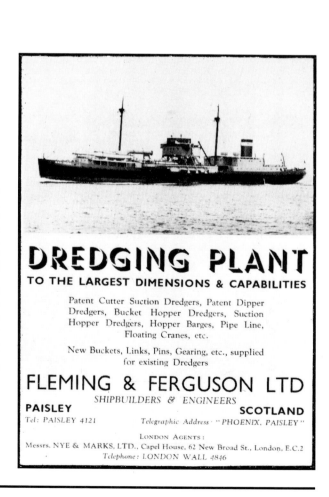

173) CONDEMNED CELL, PAISLEY JAIL c1968 — When this new Prison was declared a legal jail in August 1823, the prisoners confined in the Old Tolbooth were to be transferred there. The magistrates declared 'such a transfer shall not be deemed or taken to be an escape!' In 1825, some prisoners did escape, but only got as far as nearby County Square, where they stumbled across the 79th Regiment on Church Parade! They all neatly returned to their cells closing their doors behind them. The condemned cell saw two of its occupants, Craig and Brown, executed on 29 October 1829 for common theft. In 1837, William Perry was the occupant. He had murdered his wife using a saw file ground into a bayonet. Before his execution, according to the Church Authorities, he was 'most penitent'.

174) THE PAISLEY ROCKETEERS 1966 — At Gleniffer, the Rocketeers celebrated their 30th anniversary to commemorate the first flight of a model rocket over the skies of Paisley in 1935. It was designed and fired by their founder John D Stewart second from right) who described its flight as 'lively but erratic'! In 1937, he successfully launched the world's first 3-stage model rocket (now preserved in Edinburgh's Museum of Childhood). In 1938, he launched Britain's first photographic rocket! In 1979, the Rocketeers designed and fired their 'aquajets' to carry 'special mail' – now avidly collected world-wide by philatelists.

175) GEORGE STREET/CANAL STREET REDEVELOPMENT c1959 — A plan approved in 1953 to redevelop six old areas of the town began with the demolition of some 800 houses situated at West Buchanan Street, Sir Michael Street, Barr Street, Barclay Street, Canal Street and George Street. To Paisley goes the honour of first implementing the 1947 Town and Country Planning (Scotland) Act. Paisley's first high rise flats sits between George Street on the left and the new as yet incomplete inner ring road; Canal Street on the right.

176) BROWN & POLSON DISASTER, 5th June 1964 — This was the tragic scene at the Braids Road entrance of the Royal Starch Works. The large building to the rear – the animal feed plant – had been completely destroyed in a huge explosion at about 6.40am that morning. Workers, who had arrived for the 6.45am shift, had to run for their lives. Local firemen, ambulancemen and workers tore at the rubble to search for casualties. Anxious relatives stood around waiting news. Four men were killed, four were badly injured, and one was never found. A local policeman described the scene 'I have seen terrible scenes during the war, but never anything like this'.

177) THOMAS WHITE & SONS LTD LAIGHPARK, ABERCORN STREET — This company was founded for the production of woodworking machinery. The photograph shows the assembly line for their renowned wide-belt sanding machines. The company was founded in 1863 by Thomas White and specialised in spool and bobbin making machines and textile machinery for the Paisley thread industry. In the early twenties, the decision was taken to specialise in making woodworking machinery, and over a period of twenty years many patents were granted for novel applications. In the 1960s, the company was the third largest manufacturer of woodworking machinery in Britain, and known throughout the world for their planing and sanding machines. It was closed by J & P Coats' in the 1970s.

178) PAISLEY MALE VOICE CHOIR 1970 — The Paisley Male Voice Choir was formed in 1943, under the leadership of Farquhar Macdonald their conductor, who emerged from the ranks of the famous Glasgow Orpheus Choir. The Choir can boast of two major recordings made in 1973 and 1976. Their repertoire is wide ranging from humble folk songs to operatic works. Through radio and television and recent performances in Glasgow Royal Concert Hall, they have become Paisley's ambassadors of song, their audiences are asked to lend an ear to Paisley as well as keeping an eye on it! The Choir is ably led today by their conductor George Gray.

179) COUNTY BUILDINGS AND JAIL c1968 — This magnificent group of floodlit buildings featured in the town's post-war Christmas lights. A proposal to have it demolished in 1939 was postponed because of the war. The old buildings, containing the town's offices, the Police HQ and a jail, finally became redundant with the opening of the new municipal buildings at Cotton Street in 1969. It was also in the way of a new shopping complex to be called the 'Piazza' and was therefore demolished in 1971!

180) THE PIAZZA/COUNTY SQUARE 1970 — Paisley's most dramatic and irreversible act of town-centre clearance took place between 1969 and 1971. The old County Buildings and Jail, stretching between County Place and the River Cart, were demolished; the Cart covered over; and a new shopping/office precinct built. Here we see the stumps of the walls of the old Burgh Chambers just prior to their final removal. Behind rises the multi-storey car park not long erected to serve the 'Piazza' and towering over Gilmour Street Station on the left. The only remnant of the 'swinging sixties' in the picture is the girl sporting a mini-skirt!

181) STORIE STREET CATTLE MARKET c. 1970 — In 1874, sales of cattle were held in the yard of the Bull Inn, New Street, but, as turnover increased, Storie Street market was opened up a few years later. This market attracted considerable trade to the town from the influx of country folk. One character in particular who often appeared here was 'Flannel Jaws', a cattle drover. He got his nickname because he always wore a large piece of grey flannel wrapped over his head and tied under his chin. During the 1950s and 60s it was a common sight to see escaped bulls or sheep running down the High Street, chased by schoolboys and policemen and causing hilarious scenes at the Cross. The market left Storie Street and moved to Glenfield in 1971.

182) PAISLEY ABBEY RESTORED CHOIR 1982 — For centuries, the choir lay in ruins but by 1928 it had been completely restored. The magnificent vaulted stone ceiling, its chief glory, had been originally designed by McGregor Chalmers, however the work of restoration, had at the time of his death, in 1922, only reached to the top of the choir walls. His cousin and successor, Sir Robert Lorimer, discovered that the springers for the vaulted roof had been incorrectly set out. He set his assistant, A G Lochhead, the task of redesigning it. The contractor, who carried out all this magnificent work, was William & John Taylor of Possilpark. Below the banners of local regiments in the choir, are the burial places of King Robert III, the two wives of Robert II, Princess Marjory Bruce, and the first six High Stewards of Scotland.

183) CRAWFORD W. FAIRBROTHER M.B.E. (1936-1986) —
Born in Paisley to a father who had been twice runner-up Scottish
High Jump Champion. As a pupil of the John Neilson Institution,
he won the Scottish Schoolboys High Jump Championship in
1955. He became Scottish Champion between 1957 and 1969 a
record 13 times. In full internationals, he was 'capped' 53 times.
In 1959 he broke the British record at Rome by clearing 2.05m,
and was the first Briton to clear 2m indoors. He also appeared as
Scottish Captain at three out of four Commonwealth Games
between 1958-1970. At the last of these 1970 Games, held in
Edinburgh, he was given the distinction of taking the Oath for the
competitors – a fitting tribute in the twilight of an illustrious
athletics career. In 1962, as British Champion, he was honoured
with a civic reception by Paisley Town Council and presented
with an inscribed silver salver. Like all great sportsmen, he was
a sound technician who preferred the 'Straddle' as opposed to the
'Fosbury Flop', totally committed to his sport, yet found time for
his family, his golf and cricket, and for his loyal support of St.
Mirren FC.

184) DR WHO EXHIBITION, November 1988 — To commemorate the 25th year of 'Dr. Who', the Paisley Branch of the
Dr Who Appreciation Society mounted an exhibition of memorabilia in Paisley Museum. The exhibition proved very
popular, as can be seen by the numbers of excited fans seeing Dr Who (Sylvester McCoy) confronting a Dalek!

185) ST MIRREN FC 1987 — St Mirren won the Scottish Cup for only the third time, beating Dundee United 1-0 in the final, to bring back the coveted trophy. An excited crowd of five thousand supporters had gathered outside the Town Hall to welcome the victorious team. Even the statues, trees and lampposts became perches for happy supporters! When Jimmy Bone saluted the crowd from the balcony of the Town Hall and shouted, 'Paisley! Paisley!', a great roar went up. It was fitting that Bone, then the Assistant Manager, should hold up the trophy, as he had led the team to another celebrated victory in 1980, when they won the Anglo-Scottish Cup.

186) QUEEN'S VISIT AUGUST 1988 — Paisley Buddies turned out in their thousands to welcome Queen Elizabeth and Prince Philip who were visiting the town to commemorate the Paisley 500 celebration. The Queen's first stop was at Paisley Museum, where she opened a local history exhibition. From the Museum the royal party drove down the High Street, and at Dunn Square the Queen planted a Paisley 500 anniversary rose. The Queen and Prince Philip then walked to Paisley Abbey, for a commemorative service. This picture shows the royal party leaving the Abbey, by the great West doorway, prior to officially opening the new Lagoon Centre.

187) MARJORY BRUCE CAIRN 1991 — This modern cairn erected in Renfrew Road claims to mark the locality where Princess Marjory Bruce, wrongly called 'Queen Blearie', ancestor of the Royal House of Stewart, fell from her horse in 1317 and broke her neck. As she was in an advanced state of pregnancy, her son, who became King Robert II, was miraculously saved by Caesarean birth. This myth can not be substantiated. Near the present day monument, an older monument in existence in 1772, now lost, and known as Queen Blearie's Cross marked the likely site of the Battle of Renfrew fought in 1164; 'Cuine Blair' signifying a 'memorial of battle'.

188) SMA' SHOT PARADE PAISLEY CROSS 1991 — Since July 1986, a replica of the Charleston Drum has led a costumed procession through the town to celebrate the Sma' Shot holiday. The sma' shot used by the Paisley shawl weavers was a binding shot of fine lace cotton used to reinforce the fabric of a shawl. It was an essential part of the shawl, but as it was not seen on the finished surface, the employers, or 'Corks', refused to reimburse the weavers for the extra cost of the material. About 1856, after a long struggle against this injustice, the weavers eventually won, and in celebration named their existing holiday 'Sma' Shot Day'. The Charleston drum (reputedly carried at Waterloo), the symbol of the Charleston weavers, was used to call out weavers on strife.

189) BURNING THE CORK ABBEY CLOSE July 1991 — A crowd of five thousand people had gathered in Abbey Close to witness the 'burning of the Cork' – the climax of Paisley's 'Sma' Shot' Parade. The 'Cork' was the employer of the weavers in Paisley. 'Burning the Cork' is recorded in Charleston in 1835. The old radical weavers of this village, due to a dispute over payment for work done, hung an effigy of their employer in the street. After this it was carried shoulder high by a large crowd, accompanied by a band, through the streets of Paisley. On arriving at the employer's house, and after breaking his windows and assailing the inhabitants with abuse, the effigy was burnt.

190) COATS MEMORIAL CHURCH 1992 — Thomas Coats died in 1883, having been a life-long member of Storie Street Baptist Church. This Church was built in his memory by the Coats family and opened in 1894. The Church took nine years to complete. The architect of this magnificent Gothic revival building was Hippolyte Blanc RSA, a Belgian architect based in Edinburgh. He had two large scale design models made for approval, both eight feet long and illuminated by electricity. The design chosen was the church with the crown spire. The sheer scale and setting of this Baptist Church is astonishing and must surely rank as one of the finest churches built in Europe, during the nineteenth century.

191) GREENLAW HOUSE, MANSIONHOUSE ROAD 1992 — This country mansion once belonged to Robert Corse (1701-1777), a rich Paisley merchant. This house, erected in 1774, on the top of Greenlaw Hill, was described in 1781 as, 'being finished in the completest manner; of good ashlar work, and the stones polished, adorned with an Ionic cornice and a concave door built after the Corinthian order fronting the west, balustraded on the top, crowned with vases.' The two square wings had leaded roofs with Venetian windows. A tower-of-the-Winds portico and centre bay window were added around 1840. The coachhouse serving the house, built in rococo gothic can still be seen nearby. The mansionhouse is now private flats.

192) PAISLEY COLLEGE OF TECHNOLOGY, GEORGE STREET 1992 — This College was founded in 1897 as Paisley Technical College and School of Art. The old Government School of Design in Gilmour Street was incorporated into the new college. Peter Brough (1797-1883), a local business man, had, in 1879, left funds to establish and maintain a science lectureship in Paisley. Those funds were used mainly in the building of the college. From its inception, the College was dependant on local industries. This successful policy bore fruit, as in 1950 it became a Central Institution. In the 1960s, the College expanded greatly. In 1966, its first degree and honour courses were started. Between 1972-74 major additions were erected. In 1992 it was announced it is to become the University of Paisley.

193) THE PAISLEY CENTRE 1993 — After many years of planning, the town's new indoor shopping mall was officially opened on 19 June 1992 by HRH The Princess of Wales. This large complex on three levels links with the shopping thoroughfares of High Street, Causeyside Street and New Street. The High Street entrance retains the facade of the old Picture House; the Causeyside entrance, the frontage of the old Paisley Co-operative Society; and at New Street, the Paisley Arts Centre nestles on two sides of this large modern complex. The view shows the mall leading towards the High Street.

194) PAISLEY ICE RINK, February 1993 — Between 1970 and 1992, Paisley had no ice rink. This new complex more than meets the town's needs in skating and curling facilities. Once again the 'Paisley Pirates', its new ice hockey team, takes on the mantle of its illustrious predecessors, and once again ice hockey plays to a packed arena. This new ice rink has already been favoured by a visit of Torvill and Dean, the ice dance stars.

195) MEDIEVAL DRAIN PAISLEY ABBEY 1992 — Although the drain running under the old grounds of the Abbey was known and described in the late Victorian period, it is only within the last year or so that it was re-opened. This rediscovered drain, arguably the finest of its type in Scotland to have survived from medieval times, is beautifully built in stone, and has a vaulted roof. With it's tunnel-like appearance the sewer gave rise to the legend, known to every Paisley schoolchild, 'that a tunnel ran from Paisley Abbey to Crookston Castle or Stanely Castle'!

196) PAISLEY TERRIER — At the back of the painting stands the Paisley Terrier. Bred in Paisley and district during the eighteenth century, the breed was popular with the town's textile workers for ridding the workshops and warehouses of troublesome and costly vermin. Like its Paisley masters, it was short in the back, very tough, a magnificent fighter and afraid of nothing! It survived as a breed in Britain until 1927 but may still survive in the USA. However, its descendant of today, the Yorkshire Terrier, still displays some of the original Paisley characteristics.

197) PAISLEY CROSS 1992 — The statues of Sir Peter Coats and his brother, Thomas, have been standing and watching over their old town, since 1889 and are a fitting tribute to the town's two greatest benefactors. Behind rises the magnificent riverside facade of the Clark Town Hall, a reminder that the Clark family, who donated it to the town, could not be outdone in magnanimity, by their old trade arch-rivals the Coats!

198) PROCESSION OF DIOGENES April 1992 — Alexander Stoddart, the Paisley sculptor, was commissioned to make a statue of the Ancient Greek philosopher, Diogenes for the hall of the John Neilson Institution, a school now converted to flats. The dome of the building, locally known as the 'Parritch Bowl', is an outstanding landmark on the Paisley skyline. In the tradition of the classical sculptors, the statue was carried through the streets for the public to see. The sculptor can just be seen looking up at his statue, as it is carried along Oakshaw, past Coat's Observatory. Note the 'wee parritch bowl' in Diogene's hand.

SELECT BIBLIOGRAPHY

BOOKS: *Witch Hunt* – I. Adam; *The Story of Paisley* – C. Stewart Black; *The Paisley Shawl, The Paisley Thread* – M. Blair; *History of Paisley, Paisley Burns Club, Paisley Poets, History of the Paisley Grammar School* – Robert Brown; *Paisley, a History* – S. Clark; *A General Description of the Shire of Renfrew, Editions 1710* – Crawford, *1782* – Crawford & Semple, *1818* – Crawford & Robertson; *Alexander Wilson* – T. Crichton; *The Witches of Renfrewshire* – A. Gardner; *Judicial Records of Renfrewshire, Vanduara or Odds and Ends* – W. Hector; *Paisley Abbey* – A. R. Howell; *The Life and Letters of Alexander Wilson* – C. Hunter; *Sanitation in Paisley* – W. Kelso; *Abbey of Paisley* – J. C. Lees; *A Social Geography of Paisley* – M. McCarthy; *Yesterday's Paisley, Recollections of Paisley* – D. Malcolm; *Let Paisley Flourish, John Henning* – John Malden; *Abbey and Town of Paisley* – C. Mackie; *History of Paisley, Lordship of Paisley, Burgh of Paisley - Charters and Documents* – W. M. Metcalfe; *History of Paisley, The Life and Opinions of Arthur Sneddon, A Betheral's Life* – John Parkhill, *The Paisley Pattern, Paisley Patterns* – V. Reilly; *Old Houses, Old Families and Olden Times in Paisley, Tannahill's Songs and Poems, Paisley Town's House, St. Mirin and Supplements* – David Semple: *Statistical Accounts of Scotland, 1793, 1845 and 1962, The South Clyde Estuary* – Dr. Frank Walker; *The American Ornithology* – A. Wilson.
NEWSPAPERS AND MAGAZINES: The Paisley Advertiser; The Paisley Daily Express; Paisley Herald; Renfrewshire Independent; Paisley Journal; The Paisley Magazine 1828; The Paisley Portfolio 1895; Renfrewshire Gazette; The Renfrewshire Magazine 1846-47.
DIRECTORIES: Hinshalwood; Fowler; Pigot Trade Directories of Paisley.